CITIES IN THE COMMONWEALTH

Two Centuries of Urban Life in Kentucky

ALLEN J. SHARE

THE UNIVERSITY PRESS OF KENTUCKY

Copyright © 1982 by The University Press of Kentucky
Paperback edition 2009

The University Press of Kentucky
Scholarly publisher for the Commonwealth, serving Bellarmine University, Berea College, Centre College of Kentucky, Eastern Kentucky University, The Filson Historical Society, Georgetown College, Kentucky Historical Society, Kentucky State University, Morehead State University, Murray State University, Northern Kentucky University, Transylvania University, University of Kentucky, University of Louisville, and Western Kentucky University.
All rights reserved.

Editorial and Sales Offices: The University Press of Kentucky
663 South Limestone Street, Lexington, Kentucky 40508-4008
www.kentuckypress.com

Cover illustration: View of Main Street, Louisville, in 1846
Frontispiece: Downtown Louisville, 1981

Photo credits
Cover: Lewis Collins, *Historical Sketches of Kentucky* (1847) (National Archives); frontispiece: Billy Davis, in C. Thomas Hardin, ed., *Over Kentucky: 40 Years of Aerial Photography by Billy Davis* (1981); p. x: Dunn Collection, Kentucky Historical Society Library; p. 10: William Henry Perrin, ed., *History of Fayette County, Kentucky* (1882); p. 24: William Bullock, *Sketch of a Journey Through the Western States of North America* (1827); p. 32 top: University of Louisville Art Collection; p. 32 bottom: J. C. G. Kennedy, ed., *The Progress of the Republic* (1856) (Prints and Photographs Div., Library of Congress); p. 53: Prints and Photographs Div., Library of Congress; p. 55: *Ballou's Pictorial Drawing-Room Companion* (1856); p. 78: Caufield and Shook Collection, University of Louisville Photographic Archives; p. 84 top: *Souvenir of Middlesborough, October, 1890* (1890) (Special Collections, King Library, University of Kentucky; p. 84 bottom: R. G. Potter Collection, University of Louisville Photographic Archives; p. 98: Janet E. Kemp, *Report of the Tenement House Commission of Louisville* (1909); p. 104: *Louisville Defender*; p. 116: courtesy of Robert S. Whitney; p. 124: Billy Davis, 1980; p. 130: Billy Davis, 1971.

Cataloging-in-Publication Data is available from
the Library of Congress.

ISBN 978-0-8131-9280-2 (pbk: acid-free paper)

This book is printed on acid-free recycled paper meeting
the requirements of the American National Standard
for Permanence in Paper for Printed Library Materials.

Manufactured in the United States of America.

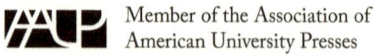 Member of the Association of American University Presses

The Kentucky Bicentennial Bookshelf
Sponsored by

KENTUCKY HISTORICAL EVENTS CELEBRATION COMMISSION
KENTUCKY FEDERATION OF WOMEN'S CLUBS

and Contributing Sponsors

AMERICAN FEDERAL SAVINGS & LOAN ASSOCIATION
ARMCO STEEL CORPORATION, ASHLAND WORKS
A. ARNOLD & SON TRANSFER & STORAGE CO., INC. / ASHLAND OIL, INC.
BAILEY MINING COMPANY, BYPRO, KENTUCKY / BEGLEY DRUG COMPANY
J. WINSTON COLEMAN, JR. / CONVENIENT INDUSTRIES OF AMERICA, INC.
IN MEMORY OF MR. AND MRS. J. SHERMAN COOPER BY THEIR CHILDREN
CORNING GLASS WORKS FOUNDATION / MRS. CLORA CORRELL
THE COURIER-JOURNAL AND THE LOUISVILLE TIMES
COVINGTON TRUST & BANKING COMPANY
MR. AND MRS. GEORGE P. CROUNSE / GEORGE E. EVANS, JR.
FARMERS BANK & CAPITAL TRUST COMPANY / FISHER-PRICE TOYS, MURRAY
MARY PAULINE FOX, M.D., IN HONOR OF CHLOE GIFFORD
MARY A. HALL, M.D., IN HONOR OF PAT LEE,
JANICE HALL & MARY ANN FAULKNER
OSCAR HORNSBY INC. / OFFICE PRODUCTS DIVISION IBM CORPORATION
JERRY'S RESTAURANTS / ROBERT B. JEWELL
LEE S. JONES / KENTUCKIANA GIRL SCOUT COUNCIL
KENTUCKY BANKERS ASSOCIATION / KENTUCKY COAL ASSOCIATION, INC.
THE KENTUCKY JOCKEY CLUB, INC. / THE LEXINGTON WOMAN'S CLUB
LINCOLN INCOME LIFE INSURANCE COMPANY
LORILLARD A DIVISION OF LOEW'S THEATRES, INC.
METROPOLITAN WOMAN'S CLUB OF LEXINGTON / BETTY HAGGIN MOLLOY
MUTUAL FEDERAL SAVINGS & LOAN ASSOCIATION
NATIONAL INDUSTRIES, INC. / RAND MCNALLY & COMPANY
PHILIP MORRIS, INCORPORATED / MRS. VICTOR SAMS
SHELL OIL COMPANY, LOUISVILLE
SOUTH CENTRAL BELL TELEPHONE COMPANY
SOUTHERN BELLE DAIRY CO. INC.
STANDARD OIL COMPANY (KENTUCKY)
STANDARD PRINTING CO., H.M. KESSLER, PRESIDENT
STATE BANK & TRUST COMPANY, RICHMOND
THOMAS INDUSTRIES INC. / TIP TOP COAL CO., INC.
MARY L. WISS, M.D. / YOUNGER WOMAN'S CLUB OF ST. MATTHEWS

Contents

Preface vii

1 / Cities in the Wilderness 1

2 / Urban Imperialism and Rivalry 22

3 / The First Urban Crisis 46

4 / Visions of Metropolis 66

5 / Segregation and Social Control 88

6 / Crucible of Culture 109

7 / Change and Continuity 123

Bibliographical Note 141

Index 148

*To RUTH SHARE
and to the memory
of OSCAR SHARE*

Preface

SEVERAL YEARS AGO the University Press of Kentucky asked me to prepare an "essay on urban Kentucky" for inclusion in its Bicentennial Bookshelf series. Accepting this invitation, I had to develop a concept to govern the work as a whole, since no model existed for writing the urban history of a single state, and to devise a way to handle a very broad topic within the confines of a book of modest proportions.

Rather than attempt to survey the entire subject lightly, I decided to write in some detail about several themes central to the process of urbanization and to the character of city life: promotion or "boosterism" and rivalry, urban problems and services, cultural life, and the black urban experience. I used these themes to structure each of the chapters, which I planned as more or less independent interpretive essays, and to guide my selection of evidence and my choice of illustrative examples.

I further decided to focus the essays primarily upon episodes in the history of Lexington and Louisville. The Bluegrass city was the largest urban center in Kentucky from the late eighteenth century until the 1820s, while after 1830 Louisville reigned as the premier city in the state. As the largest cities in the Commonwealth during the pioneer and modern periods, Lexington and Louisville were also the most important. They were, for example, the only cities to have attained the necessary size, wealth, and talent to produce significant cultural achievements. In other areas of urban life, moreover, cities had tended to follow similar patterns, and it seemed appropriate in a concise work to concentrate on the course of events in Kentucky's major cities and to allude to related developments in other communities.

One writer defined an essay as "a piece of writing principally for reflection and the recharging of the brain." Another suggested that a series of essays should be put together "like organizing a meal. The various dishes must be so arranged as to rouse the appetite and renew the pleasure with each course." If this volume of essays measures up to such standards of the genre, it will have fulfilled one of its primary objectives. It will have fulfilled another if the individual essays raise at least as many questions as they answer, provide some guidelines for further investigation, and encourage others to explore the rich yet neglected urban history of Kentucky.

In any piece of historical writing, one accumulates a number of debts to one's colleagues. In a work of synthesis, the extent of those debts is far greater than usual. I have indicated in the Bibliographical Note the authors to whom I am most deeply indebted, but it is impossible to acknowledge adequately the many colleagues and scholars upon whose work I have drawn and relied. Without the careful labors of my fellow historians the present work could never have been written.

The following historians kindly permitted me to read their unpublished manuscripts and work in progress: Leonard P. Curry of the University of Louisville, Nancy Schrom Dye of the University of Kentucky, Judith Walzer Leavitt of the University of Wisconsin, Lee Shai Weissbach of the University of Louisville, and George C. Wright of the University of Texas. Robert S. Whitney, conductor emeritus of the Louisville Orchestra, allowed me to read the drafts of his unpublished history of the orchestra.

My good friends Steven A. Channing of the Department of History of the University of Kentucky and James C. Anderson of the University of Louisville's Photographic Archives carefully read the entire manuscript and offered thoughtful comments and suggestions. Steve gave me the benefit of his expertise in the areas of Kentucky and American history, and Andy helped me select photographs to accompany the text.

Ann Taylor Allen of the Department of History of the University of Louisville encouraged the undertaking from the beginning, listened to my ideas as the project evolved, read successive drafts of the various chapters, and provided wise counsel on substantive and stylistic matters. She was at all times the best of colleagues and the best of friends.

My students in the School of Medicine of the University of Louisville cheered me throughout the many weeks and weekends spent writing and revising these pages, and I thank them for being such good colleagues and companions and for making me glad each year that I became a teacher.

I also thank the University of Louisville's Committee on Academic Publication for providing funds to help defray the costs of securing illustrations.

My typist prepared the manuscript with the loving care and the attention to detail usually reserved for one's own work—which, in this case, it happened to be.

Scholarly convention obliges me to declare that I am solely responsible for errors of fact or interpretation. Yet, as William Camden observed in 1637, "it may be that I have been misled by the credit of authors and others whom I tooke to be most true, and worthy of credit. . . . Others may be more skilfull and more exactly observe the particularities of the places where they are conversant; if they, or any other, whosoever, will advertise mee wherein I am mistaken, I will amend it with manifold thankes . . . if it proceed from good meaning, and not from a spirit of contradiction and quarrelling, which doe not befit such as are well bred, and affect the truth."

Mid-nineteenth-century Lexington as seen from Transylvania University

1

CITIES IN THE WILDERNESS

IN 1773 THE WILDERNESS that would later become the Commonwealth of Kentucky lay virtually untouched, inviting yet menacing. "Odds were indeed great in 1773 against a settlement being planted in Kentucky," historian Thomas D. Clark observed. "It was still too far in advance of the spreading line of civilization for safety." But in August of that very year, hundreds of miles beyond the line of settlement, Captain Thomas Bullitt of Virginia and his small party were encamped just above the Falls of the Ohio on the south bank of the river, busily surveying land and laying out a town for speculator John Connolly. Having received a 2,000-acre grant of land at the falls for his services to the British crown during the French and Indian War, Connolly took entrepreneur John Campbell as a partner and the two advertised the sale of lots in their projected city in April 1774. Their exuberant proclamation of preordained metropolitan destiny heralded the birth of urban promotion and boosterism in the Ohio and Mississippi valleys. "The advantageous situation of that place, formed by nature as a . . . repository to receive the produce of the very extensive and fertile country on the Ohio and its branches, . . . is sufficient to recommend it," they exclaimed; "but when it is considered how liberal, nay profuse, nature has been to it otherwise in stocking it so abundantly that the slightest industry may supply the most numerous family with the greatest plenty . . . we may with certainty affirm that it will in a short time be equalled by few inland places on the American continent." The outbreak of the American Revolution together with Indian unrest forced Connolly and Campbell to abandon their efforts. Yet, however tenuously—and months before James Harrod's tiny expedition established the first permanent Anglo-American settlement in the trans-Appalachian West—these two town promoters had planted the seeds of an urban civilization in the future state of Kentucky.

From the earliest days of settlement in Kentucky, as elsewhere in the Ohio Valley, the planting of cities at strategic military and commercial sites along the banks of major waterways and in the hearts of fertile farming districts was a vital economic and social activity. As historian Richard C. Wade demonstrated, these young towns functioned as "spearheads of the frontier," driving a wedge of urbanity into the raw wilderness and serving as bases that held the region in advance of intensive agricultural settlement. In his memoir on the late eighteenth-century mainsprings of trans-Appalachian development, Daniel Drake, a prominent physician and one of the foremost citizens of early nineteenth-century Cincinnati, Louisville, and Lexington, commented on the crucial role of cities in frontier life. "It is worthy of remark, that those who made these beginnings of settlement projected towns, which they anticipated would grow into cities," Drake reflected. "And we may see in their origins one of the elements of the prevalent tendency to rear up towns in advance of the country. . . . The followers of the first pioneers, like themselves, had a taste for commerce and the mechanic arts which cannot be gratified without the construction of cities." Like many others who moved to the Ohio Valley in search of opportunities in promising young cities, Drake equated urbanization with progress and envisioned a West of great cities. "It will perhaps, to many persons appear altogether visionary, if not boastful to speak of *cities* on these western waters," he wrote in 1815. "Yet it is certain . . . that many of the villages which have sprung up within 30 years, on the banks of the Ohio and Mississippi are destined, before the termination of the present century, to attain the rank of populous and magnificent cities."

That nature had ordained a future great city at the Falls of the

Ohio had been recognized by explorers, hunters, and traders for at least a century before a permanent community was established there. From the beginnings of colonial urban settlement, when cities were founded to serve the needs of a mercantilist empire, the exigencies of commerce dictated city location—at the mouths of magnificent harbors, at the junctures of major navigable rivers, at natural breaks in trade. The Falls of the Ohio, a violent stretch of rapids created by a fossilized coral reef running obliquely across the river, was the only significant obstacle to navigation along the entire course of the Ohio and Mississippi rivers from the headwaters to the Gulf of Mexico. There the river dropped twenty-two feet in a distance of two miles, making passage dangerous at high water and all but impossible most of the year. "The ear is stunned with the sound of rushing waters," tourist James Hall remarked, "and the sight of waves dashing, and foaming, and whirling among the rocks and eddies below, is grand and fearful." Vessels had to put in at either end of this "boiling place" and transfer passengers and freight to overland carriers, thus insuring the rise of a city to serve as a transshipment point.

Four years after Connolly and Campbell's enterprise collapsed, a permanent community was established at the Falls of the Ohio—the first settlement along the lower reaches of the Ohio River and the remotest outpost of American settlement during the War for Independence. In May 1778 George Rogers Clark, carrying secret orders to proceed against the British in the Old Northwest, set up a tiny military base on Corn Island, at the foot of present-day downtown Louisville. Here Clark trained his 150 soldiers, and here also the 50 civilians who had accompanied the expedition set about putting down roots. Receiving news the following year of Clark's military victories in the Illinois country, the settlers moved into another small stockade on the mainland. In April 1779 the inhabitants organized a town government, elected trustees, surveyed the site, and prepared a plan for the town. The following year the state of Virginia issued a charter which invested title to the town in the trustees, making Louisville its own proprietor. With the completion in 1782 of Fort Nelson, an imposing stronghold designed to secure the area from British or Indian depredations, the citizens began to improve and build up their town.

Despite its promising circumstances, Louisville grew slowly during the last two decades of the eighteenth century. The major obstacle to expansion proved to be the terrifying menace posed by the Indians. In April 1781 resident John Floyd wrote to the governor of Virginia describing the perils he and others faced in the infant community. "We are all obliged to live in our forts in this country, and notwithstanding all the caution we use, forty-seven . . . have been killed or taken prisoners by the savages, besides a number wounded, since January. Whole families are destroyed without regard to age or sex; infants are torn from their mothers arms and their brains dashed out against trees. . . . Not a week passes, and some weeks scarcely a day, without some of our distressed inhabitants feeling the fatal effects of the infernal rage and fury of these execrable hell-hounds." Throughout the 1780s the Indians continued to "infest the roads," while immigrants traveling on the river came in flatboats with high sides designed to block Indian arrows.

Almost as serious as the Indian peril was the problem of disease and ill health, which early gave Louisville an unsavory reputation as the "Graveyard of the West." Stagnant pools of water dotted the low, marshy landscape, giving rise to epidemic yellow fever as well as to endemic malaria. Visitor William Winterbotham suggested in 1795 that Louisville's "unhealthiness . . . has considerably retarded its growth," while a decade later traveler Thomas Ashe complained about the "character of unhealthiness in the place, which forbids the encouragement of any hope of its permanency or improvement." Yet most commentators agreed with Pennsylvanian Josiah Espy, who in 1805 wrote that "it is to be presumed that its great natural advantages will finally get the better of the prejudices now existing against it on account of its being so sickly, and that it will yet . . . become a great and flourishing town."

A third condition retarding Louisville's early growth was the difficulty of upriver travel during the age of keelboats, flatboats, and barges. The trip up the Mississippi and Ohio rivers from New Orleans to Louisville consumed between three and four months, while the journey from the Falls City to Pittsburgh required an additional month. A crew of twenty to thirty strong men had to use every device then known to overcome the obstacles to upstream navigation. They poled the river bottom when it was solid, used sails on wide expanses of water, rowed, hauled their craft forward by means of heavy ropes tied to trees, and even resorted to "bushwhacking," grasping bushes or branches of trees in order to pull the boat up the river. The slow and arduous upstream voyage kept freight rates high, and upriver traffic averaged a mere tenth of downriver commerce. During the 1780s and 1790s trade also suffered from restrictive Spanish policies which effectively closed the Mississippi River and the port of New Orleans to American commerce. In 1800 the census counted only 359 inhabitants in the town, although travelers estimated the population at about 800, and Louisville lagged behind Lexington and Pittsburgh among the West's young cities.

Despite such formidable obstacles to growth, the citizens of Louisville early created an enclave of culture and urbanity in the backwoods. Hector St. John de Crevecoeur, the French-born essayist and author of *Letters from an American Farmer,* registered his shock at the speed with which the amenities of urban life were springing up in the tiny outpost. As his boat drew close to shore in August 1784 Crevecoeur noticed that the male passengers on a nearby vessel wore silk stockings and that the women flaunted parasols. "What was my surprise when, in place of the huts, the tents, and the primitive cabins . . . I saw numerous houses of two stories, elegant and well painted, and (as far as the stumps of trees would permit) that all the streets were spacious and well laid out," he exclaimed. "The sight of this suggestive gradation of houses finished, imperfect, just commenced, of cabins built against the trees; the aspect of the cradle of this young city, destined by its situation to become the metropolis of the surrounding country—all these objects impress me with a reverence and respect that I cannot well define. . . . Never before have I experienced that feeling which ought, it seems to me, to attend those who are actively engaged in founding a great settlement or a new city, and which should compensate them for their troubles and privations. . . . What movement, what activity, on this little theater of Louisville!"

The pulse of the young town beat to a mercantile tempo, and

the small but growing volume of commerce provided a measure of prosperity and a basis for future expansion. Situated at the head of ascending and the foot of descending navigation on the Ohio, Louisville served as a regional distributing center for the flour, hemp, pork, tobacco, and other staple products being shipped south to New Orleans, and for the cotton, sugar, rice, seafood, and imported luxury items being shipped north from the Crescent City. The need to unload, transfer, and reload all goods at the falls stimulated the growth of a thriving portaging business for wagon masters and draymen, which in turn spurred the development of busy warehousing concerns and a booming wholesale trade. As the first American port that traders reached from New Orleans, Louisville was designated a port of entry for foreign commodities and the collection of customs duties, first by Virginia in 1783 and later by Congress in 1799. Local agents insured goods shipped from the city, and wayfarers patronized the growing number of hotels, restaurants, inns, saloons, general stores, and retail establishments. By 1810 traveler John Melish could affirm that "Louisville, being the principal port of the western part of the state of Kentucky, is a market for the purchase of all kinds of produce, and the quantity that is annually shipped down the river is immense."

The thriving commerce on the Ohio and Mississippi rivers early gave rise to the building and equipping of boats and barges at the Falls of the Ohio. Other manufacturing activities began during the second decade of the nineteenth century, such as Paul Skidmore's iron foundry which opened in 1812 for the production of steam engines. Three years later the Tarascon brothers invested $150,000 in their six-story Merchant Manufacturing Mill to produce flour, and in the same year, on an equally grand scale, the Hope Distillery Company put up a huge factory in order to carry on its business "in a much more extensive mode than any hitherto established in the United States." By 1815 Louisville boasted four rope walks, an equal number of soap factories, two tobacco manufactories, a nail factory, a steam saw mill, and a stoneware factory.

There were many indications of rising prosperity and economic expansion during these years. The city's population rose to 1,357 in 1810, and doubled again during the next five years. Louisville's tax lists revealed the growing wealth of the community, as residents paid $90,550 in taxes in 1803, $189,797 in 1813, and $326,705 in 1815. Land prices soared as real estate boomed, and lots on the principal streets which had sold for $700 to $1,400 during the earlier years of settlement brought $4,000 to $5,000 by 1815. The city was assuming the air of a place of importance, and visitor Fortescue Cuming declared that "the houses [are] generally superior to any I have seen in the western country with the exception of Lexington. Most are of handsome brick, and some are three stories, with a parapet wall on the top in the modern European taste . . . I had thought Cincinnati one of the most beautiful towns I had seen in America, but Louisville, which is almost as large, equals it in beauty, and in the opinion of many excels it."

The young city offered a range of cultural activities as well as less refined amusements for the enjoyment of the growing population. Residents and visitors could watch horse races, theatrical productions, trained animal acts, and "weird dancers," play "roley-bolleys," card games, "foot-ball," and "a sober game of whist or the more scientific one of billiards," or frequent bawdy houses, barbeques, fish-feasts, wedding parties, balls, and conscription dances. British traveler Henry Bradshaw Fearon identified the polite sport of "gander pulling," a "diversion [which] consists in tying a live gander to a tree or pole, greasing its neck, riding past it at full gallop, and he who succeeds in pulling off the head of the victim, receives the laurel crown [and] the body of the gander." More decorous pastimes appeared early, such as Mr. Nickle's dancing school, which by 1786 was instructing "some 12 or 15 young misses . . . middling neatly dressed." By 1819 the city's first historian, Henry McMurtrie, could point to an emerging cultural establishment. "There is a circle, small 'tis true, but within whose magic round abounds every pleasure that wealth, regulated by taste, can produce, or urbanity bestow," he proclaimed. "There, the 'red heel' of Versailles may imagine himself in the emporium of fashion, and whilst leading a beauty through the mazes of the dance, forget that he is in the wilds of America."

Early townspeople so rapidly transformed wilderness outposts into "emporia of fashion" because they defined urbanism as, in part, a process of furnishing cultural and social amenities. As

Daniel Drake observed, many of these settlers had come from "those portions of the Union which cherish and build up cities." Evidence suggests that a large number of the people in policy-making and leadership positions in the new towns knew a great deal about life in eastern cities, from having lived in and visited them. Town builders derived their standards of urbanity from the East's oldest and largest metropolitan centers, and in everything from street plans and municipal services to cultural institutions and architectural styles, the urban frontiersmen studied, adopted, and adapted the ways and practices of Boston, New York, Baltimore, and Philadelphia.

The process by which Louisville established a public school system in 1829 clearly reflected this urge to emulate the eastern metropolises. The community's council sent the new principal, Mann Butler, "to the eastern cities, to examine the most respectable of their *monitorial* establishments." Taking detailed notes on the systems of Baltimore, Philadelphia, New York, and Boston, and declaring that his trip "will save our city funds from . . . expensive errors of others and from fruitless experiments," Butler submitted his report to the legislators, to the school's trustees, and, through the press, to the people of Louisville. The first report of the school committee indicated that the building itself was designed "mainly after the plan of the High School of New York, united with the Public School Rooms of Philadelphia." Faculty were recruited from London and from Columbia and Yale universities, while the curriculum was patterned on those of "the High School of New York and some of the Boston establishments." Even such small items as slates and lesson cards were brought back to Louisville from Philadelphia by Butler and employed in the new system. Louisvillians were proud to have set up the first free public school west of the Alleghenies, and equally proud that their achievements mirrored those in large metropolitan centers. "It is gratifying to us," the editor of the *Louisville Public Advertiser* announced, "that Louisville has the honor of taking the lead in the West, as New York did in the East, in the adoption of the monitorial system, which has been so thoroughly tried, and is now so highly approved, in London, Edinburgh, and in our sister states in the East."

While Louisville became a regional metropolis because of its location on the Ohio River, Lexington, alone among the important cities of the first West, occupied an inland position. Planted at a site within the encircling arm of the Kentucky River, Lexington was a good fifteen miles away from that artery, and the branch of Elkhorn Creek which cut through the town was far too shallow to sustain commerce. Yet Lexington was situated astride the major avenues of overland trade and migration, and it enjoyed an astonishing commercial boom for almost forty years during the heyday of the turnpike era and before the introduction of steamboats revolutionized western trade. Lexington grew and prospered as the supply depot and marketplace of the New West, outfitting travelers and pioneers, provisioning a regional hinterland with essential supplies, and distributing the area's agricultural surpluses to far-flung markets. For a brief time Lexington eclipsed its now more famous rivals and became known as the "Athens of the West"—the economic and social, legal and political, intellectual and cultural capital of the new country and its largest and wealthiest city.

Decades before the city was founded, the site it would grow upon had become a strategic focal point in the heart of the fertile Bluegrass region, the crossroads of buffalo and Indian trails. A band of hunters camped nearby in June 1775 named the place Lexington after receiving news of the opening battle of the American Revolution. But, like Louisville, Lexington had to wait four years before a permanent community could be established, primarily because of Indian attacks. In April 1779 a party of twenty-five pioneers erected cabins and a stockade. Three years later the Virginia legislature vested title to the recently laid out town in its five elected trustees, and in 1783 the first buildings outside the fort were constructed. By 1790 the town had 835 inhabitants and was generally "reckoned the capital of Kentucky." A decade later the city's population stood at 1,795, and Lexington was the largest town in western America.

During the 1780s and 1790s Lexington throve on trade, becoming the entrepôt linking Europe and the eastern states with the Ohio and Mississippi valleys. "The market-place . . . of this little metropolis . . . stretches over the whole breadth of the

The "old fort" at Lexington, built in 1782

square," traveler Alexander Wilson noted. "The numerous shops piled with goods, and the many well-dressed females I passed in the streets; the sound of social industry, and the gay scenery of 'the busy haunts of men,' had a most exhilarating effect on my spirits, after being so long immured in the forest." Fortescue Cuming reported in 1807 that twenty-two Lexington stores annually retailed more than $300,000 worth of imported foreign goods, and by 1810 the largest retail merchants did a business during the fall and winter seasons estimated at up to $100,000 a month. Entrepreneur Thomas Hart, who amassed a fortune in his extensive wholesale and retail businesses, invited his colleagues in the East to join him "in raking up Money and spending it with our friends" in Lexington.

The large and consistent profits from commerce enabled some businessmen to accumulate substantial capital reserves. The continuing unfavorable balance of trade with the East, along with the disruptions of trade both before and during the War of 1812, increasingly encouraged wealthy merchants to invest some of this capital in local industry. Large surpluses of hemp, the demand for cloth and rope in the West, and the rising market for rough cloth (called "cotton bagging") and twine in the South following the invention of the cotton gin, triggered the large-scale manufacture of cordage, bagging, and sailcloth. In 1809 John Melish, a Scottish textile manufacturer, reported that the "13 extensive ropewalks, five bagging manufactories, and one of duck[cloth]," comprising the city's principal industry, produced hempen goods worth $500,000. The chronic labor shortage, along with wartime disruptions of trade, promoted diversification during the first fifteen years of the nineteenth century. In 1810 Melish calculated that Lexington's industries had increased forty-fold over the course of the preceding decade, and by 1815 the city's workshops in the wilderness were capitalized at an estimated $2.5 million. New industries appeared so rapidly in a section of the city along the fork of the Elkhorn that residents referred to the district as "Manchester," and the community's entrepreneurs dreamed of "blowing the manufactures of Kentucky all over the Western World." Lexington's great strides in manufacturing, its substantial commerce, and its rising population, up to 4,326 by 1810 and estimated at between 6,000 and 7,000 by 1815, all bred an infectious optimism in the city's future shared by residents, visitors, and speculators alike.

Pioneer Lexington was an "instant city," transformed from outpost to metropolis in but a fraction of the time it had taken older eastern cities to mature. Samuel R. Brown, author of the widely read *Western Gazetteer,* had visited Lexington near the end of the eighteenth century and found fifty houses, "partly frame, and hewn logs, with chimneys on the *outside*," and town lots selling for thirty dollars each. Returning in 1816, he was stunned at the metamorphosis. "But how changed the scene," Brown exclaimed; "everything had assumed a new appearance. The beautiful vale of Town Fork, which in 1797, I saw variegated with cornfields, meadows and trees, had in my absence been covered with stately and elegant buildings—in short, a large and beautiful town had arisen by the creative genius of the West. The log cabins had disappeared, and in their places stood costly brick mansions, well painted and enclosed by fine yards, bespeaking the taste and wealth of their possessors. . . . The scenery around

Lexington almost equals that of the elysium of the ancients. Philadelphia, with all its surrounding beauties scarcely equals it." Land values skyrocketed, the *Kentucky Gazette* reporting in 1813 the sale of town lots "at the enormous price of $500 per foot," and *Niles' Weekly Register* noting two years later that "*town lots* sell nearly as high as in Boston, New York, Philadelphia or Baltimore, which shows that this is not a place in the wilderness, as some people suppose it to be."

Reflecting both its frontier origins and its increasing wealth and refinement, early Lexington society exhibited a curious blend of backwoods raucousness and eastern urbanity. The streets were noisy and crowded, and violence was an integral part of daily life. Irishman Thomas Ashe observed in 1806 that the community's churches "have all the glass struck out by boys in the day and the inside torn up by rogues and prostitutes who frequent them at night," while traveler Henry Franklin commented at about the same time that "the lower orders retain the faults for which they are distinguished—gaming, a love of spirituous liquors, and ferocious quarrels in consequence of intoxication." Yet by the turn of the century Lexington had assumed many of the characteristics of an established seaboard community. The trustees had by that time ordered the sheep and cow pens removed from the streets and forbidden the keeping of pet panthers. Schools of all types were thriving and offering day and evening instruction in subjects ranging from geometry and French to fencing and the dance. Transylvania Seminary had been elevated to the status of a university, the first west of the Alleghenies, with departments of law, medicine, and the arts. The city boasted several newspapers, half a dozen publishing houses, bookstores, debating and literary clubs, dramatic societies, and a public subscription library. "The progress of the useful arts and all the refinements of civilized society advance even beyond the astonishing population," resident David Meade exclaimed in 1808, and the *Kentucky Gazette* referred to Lexington as "the Goshen of this Western World." Ashe had to admit that "the inhabitants show demonstrations of civilization," but he warned that "at particular times [they] exhibit many traits that should exclusively belong to untutored savages." The poet Thomas Moore captured the contradictory essence of the young frontier metropolis when he mused: "'Tis one dull chaos, one unfertile strife / Betwixt half-polish'd and half-barbarous life."

As a commercial emporium astride the main highways of travel, Lexington experienced a high degree of transiency, which contributed to the rough-and-tumble character of the place. Jobbers, wagon masters, itinerant salesmen, merchants, boatmen, traders, and migrants constantly moved in and out of the city. This large floating population, along with numbers of restless men and women who regularly pulled up stakes, rendered Lexington's society highly volatile and unstable. The community's first city directory, published in 1806, listed the surnames of only two of the twenty-five founders of the city, and evidence suggests that less than one-third of the founders remained in Lexington all of their lives. In all, only eleven of the fifty-seven surnames borne by Lexington's first one hundred or so settlers appeared in the 1806 directory. Even accounting for death, the changing of daughters' names through marriage, and a partial and incomplete listing of residents in the city directory, the persistence rate was strikingly low. Lexington, in short, like Louisville and most other early American communities, large and small, was a loose confederation of transients unsettled by incessant movement and rapid turnover.

This movement resulted in part from the quest for greater opportunity and upward mobility, as countless westerners and transplanted easterners sought to make their fortunes in promising frontier communities. Western cities needed and attracted ambitious artisans, merchants, and craftsmen, who either possessed or wished to develop special talents and skills. The demand for workers usually exceeded the supply in Lexington and other western cities, producing high wages, good opportunities, and full employment. Chronic labor shortages often forced employers to recruit workingmen from the East with promises of better pay and rapid advancement, and *Niles' Weekly Register* reported in 1815 that "nothing seems wanting [in Lexington] but artists of all classes, especially smiths, carpenters, joiners . . . [and] cotton and wool machine makers." Most journeyman mechanics and skilled workers lived in "prosperous circumstances," owning their own houses and "driving about in their own carriages." They were constantly in demand, "the more so as the industrious journeymen very soon become masters," as John Melish observed. As young urban economies matured, occupational diversity increased, and in 1806 Lexington's first city directory listed over fifty occupations, ranging from milliner and portrait painter to tallow candler and "umbrella & chip bonnet" manufacturer. Although there were always the destitute and the needy, there was nevertheless great opportunity for ordinary workingmen to succeed and a general level of high employment and modest prosperity.

Class lines remained more flexible than in eastern cities, and movement both up and down the social ladder occurred constantly. But socioeconomic stratification appeared early in Lexington and other frontier communities, and the distinctions between classes were noticeable, acknowledged, and considered meaningful. As the amount of wealth increased, stratification became more pronounced and the elite enhanced and consolidated their positions. Lexington's assessment records indicate that in 1808 over a third of the total valuation of more than $1 million belonged to only sixteen merchants and manufacturers. In Lexington as elsewhere the wealthiest citizens provided almost all of the leadership, filling political posts as trustees, formulating community priorities and goals, and generally managing urban affairs.

Successful Lexington merchants channeled most of their surplus capital into land speculation and magnificent country estates, in order to satisfy a taste for gracious living, take advantage of the relatively cheap price of land, and avoid the high costs and uncertain returns associated with industrial development. Prosperous merchants, manufacturers, and lawyers established lavish rural retreats that became famous for their charm and conviviality. John Breckinridge hosted gatherings at his Cabell's Dale, Henry Clay presided over affairs at Ashland, and David Meade entertained fifteen to twenty guests almost every evening at his resplendent *Chaumière du Prairie*. Some of the "between fifty and sixty villas" counted by Samuel Brown in 1816 were said to resemble estates in Languedoc and Provence with their "finely cultivated fields, rich gardens, and elegant mansions." In 1814 a surprised editor Hezekiah Niles reported that "society is polished and polite, and their balls and assemblies are conducted with as much grace and ease as they are anywhere else, and the dresses at the parties are as tasty and elegant. Strange things these in the 'backwoods!'"

Strange things indeed, and contemporaries were equally startled by the rapid advances in culture and learning. "Thirty years ago we had no right to expect that literature and science would so soon appear among us," a Lexingtonian wrote in 1811. "We hardly dreamed, by this time, to have been exempted from the necessity of exciting our youth to savage warfare, by making an enemy's scalp the diploma of their merit." Two years later an Ohio Valley editor, referring to the entire West, proclaimed that "our advances in learning, as in every other kind of improvement, are altogether astonishing. We see everyday new schools established for the education of youth; our towns teem with newspapers . . . ; the number of our bookstores and presses is incessantly increasing; public libraries are instituted, societies are rising, . . . and the Muses even have their worthy and successful Votaries." Another editor exulted that "cities have arisen in the very wilderness, . . . and form in their respective states the *foci* of art and science, of wealth and information."

As early as 1795 traveler Lewis Condict declared that Lexington had already emerged as the "Philadelphia of Kentucky," and two decades later the community's position of primacy in the Commonwealth appeared to many even stronger and more secure. Already "the seat of a great commerce, and . . . many flourishing manufactures," the editor of *Niles' Weekly Register* exclaimed in 1815, Lexington "promises to be the great inland city of the western world." Few Lexingtonians had paid any attention to French visitor Victor Collot's prediction in 1796 that "as this town has no navigation it is presumed that its increase will not be great." Few seemed terribly concerned when the census returns for 1810 showed that Pittsburgh with 4,768 inhabitants had overtaken Lexington with its population of 4,326. And few worried in 1815 when the *Enterprise* made the first successful upstream voyage by a steamboat from New Orleans to Louisville in a mere twenty-five days and cut traveling time to less than half. Indeed, Lexingtonians applauded the voyage, viewed steamboat traffic on the western waters as yet another way to extend their city's commercial hinterland, and looked to the future with optimism. Very few had any idea that, in but a few short years, this transportation innovation would smash their community's economy and crush the hopes of the landlocked "Athens of the West."

Lexington and Louisville were the most successful and prominent urban enterprises in early Kentucky, but they were certainly not the only manifestations of the urge to rear up cities in the wilderness. In 1797 traveler Gilbert Imlay referred to the "rising villages" and "trading towns" of Kentucky, noting that "ten years have produced a difference in the population and comforts of this country, which to be pourtrayed in just colours would appear marvellous." By 1800 a hub of settlements had grown up in the Bluegrass region around Lexington, and several other places had been planted at sites along the Ohio River. Imlay's "rising villages" and "trading towns" all dreamed of becoming great metropolises, and, for a few at least, such dreams would become reality.

But most of the little towns and villages never fulfilled the hopes and expectations of their founders, early residents, or promoters. Some, located too close to a more powerful neighbor, were either incorporated into the metropolis or reduced to subordinate satellites of it. Thus Portland and Shippingport were annexed by Louisville, while Newport and Covington grew up in the shadow of Cincinnati. Other places, lacking the capital, entrepreneurial talent, or geographical advantages necessary to sustain a successful drive toward urban maturity, settled into patterns of slow and unimpressive growth, as did Bardstown, Georgetown, Danville, and Maysville. Small communities such as Shelbyville, Versailles, and Paris had their dreams dashed as technological changes in the means of transportation altered established commercial and migration patterns and aided other localities. Larger places could suffer a similar fate, as did Lexington, which, after a meteoric rise and brilliant heyday, reluctantly relinquished trade and enterprise to the river cities. Frankfort owed its steady growth to the decision of state legislators to bypass larger Lexington and Louisville and locate the state capital "at the great meadow on the [Kentucky] River," and smaller places benefitted from the location in them of land offices, county seats, educational institutions, religious centers, and hospitals and asylums. Still other hamlets declined after faint beginnings and disappeared entirely, their empty shacks and decaying mills the dreary signposts of the West's first ghost towns. Commerce provided the major impetus to urban growth during these early decades, and the exigencies of trade to a considerable extent determined the outline and shape of Kentucky's urban matrix.

As one western editor explained, "it requires the united influence of many individuals and various interests and the concurrence of a diversity of circumstances, to give impulse to the healthy growth of a town." Such factors as natural and locational advantages, entrepreneurial leadership, technological innovation, outside capital investment, federal land policies, and luck, all played a role in determining urban success and failure. In Louisville's ultimate victory over a handful of competing communities at the Falls of the Ohio, for example, geographical considerations proved of vital importance. Resting on a broad alluvial plain, Louisville enjoyed unobstructed access to a rich and fertile interior hinterland. Moreover, Beargrass Creek, described as "a commodious little harbour without current [which] affords a safe and useful harbour for boats," along with the calm pool of water between Corn Island and the south bank of the river, protected the keelboats, flatboats, and barges that tied up at Louisville from being sucked into the rapids. Neighboring Shippingport and Portland, located below the falls on the Kentucky shore, were victimized by the river itself, which turned southward at the foot of the rapids and cut off their hinterlands. The Indiana towns—Jeffersonville above the falls and Clarksville and New Albany below them—were similarly sealed off from the interior by the steep "knobs" that rose behind them. These places also suffered from the stronger Indian menace north of the Ohio that significantly retarded settlement in the Old Northwest. In time Louisville exploited its natural advantages to the utmost and crushed the hopes of rival claimants to hegemony at the Falls of the Ohio.

A number of the projected townsites in Kentucky never got much further than an elaborate map, a grandiose advertisement, and a gleam in a speculator's eye. For three decades before the panic of 1819 there raged in the Ohio Valley what one newspaper editor termed a "city-making mania" in which everyone went about "anticipating flourishing cities in vision, at the mouth of every creek and bayou." This "city-making mania" had its origins in Kentucky in the last years of the eighteenth century. In 1788 Jacob Myers laid off a town on Slate Creek, which he assured readers of his advertisement in the August 9, 1788, issue of the *Kentucky Gazette,* had wide streets and a "public ground, sufficient for Courthouse, Meetinghouse and Schoolhouse." In what would later become standard practice, Myers offered free "in" and "out" lots to all persons settled in the town as of July 1, 1789. "The advantages of a Town with a public road through it to the Eastern states, and Navigable waters from it to the Ohio, must be obvious to every person," he concluded. "As soon as a crop of corn is raised on said land, I will erect a Grist mill, and further intend, as soon as possible, to erect iron works and slitting mill on the waters of Slate Creek." Town booming was apparently already catching on, for in the very same issue of the *Gazette* David Leitch ran an advertisement for his proposed town on the upper Blue Licks.

In 1795 a group of speculators, probably English, began promoting sales of lots in the projected towns of Franklinville and Lystra, described in glowing terms and depicted on elaborate maps as having churches, town halls, aqueducts, piers, colleges, markets, granaries, and "places of amusement." Both were laid out on "very eligible" plans "combining everything necessary for utility and ornament," so that "no doubt can be entertained but that a rapid progress will be made in settling them." The crescents and circuses in these "backwoods baroque" plans were probably derived from the examples of London, Bath, Exeter, and other English cities. These plans contrasted with the regular grid pattern featuring straight streets crossing at right angles that had been adopted by Philadelphia and later copied by Lexington, Louisville, and most of the other major Ohio Valley cities. The town of Lystra was laid out on the south creek of the Rolling Fork of the Salt River, with streets to be 100 feet wide and, anticipating the later common practice, free lots to be given to the first schoolmaster, the president of a college, the first member of Congress, and the first senator. The promoters had equally high hopes for Franklinville, described as "most commodiously situated between two capital branches of that fine river which gives name to the state."

Both Lystra and Franklinville were advertised in William Winterbotham's massive four-volume work entitled *An Historical, Geographical, Commercial, and Philosophical View of the United States of America, and of the European Settlements in America and the West-Indies,* published in 1796. Winterbotham also publicized a proposed city with the lyrical name Ohiopiomingo, which he said "is to contain upwards of a thousand houses, forty-three streets, a circus and several capital squares, which will be embellished with various suitable and handsome structures." This adventure in town booming was promoted by Pennsylvania financier, entrepreneur, and land speculator John Nicholson, who had agents in London to encourage settlers from England, Ireland, and Wales to emigrate to his town. The promoters exclaimed that "Ohiopiomingo, now forming, will be a most capital township and town very advantageously situated about 20 miles from Lystra and 30 miles below Louisville, on the river Ohio, . . . containing upwards of 100,000 acres of prime land, named in compliment to Piomingo, one of the Indian chiefs, a man greatly beloved and respected." Settlers lured to Ohiopiomingo found themselves beset with rival land claims, and the proposed metropolis, like Lystra and Franklinville, looked impressive only on paper. Indeed, many a naive investor in western property discovered to his dismay that he had purchased an underwater lot in a "city" which existed only in the imagination of an overzealous promoter or in the scheme of an unscrupulous swindler. Many of these speculative ventures came to nothing, and one Ohio Valley editor argued that "town making has not generally proved profitable. Of the vast number of towns which have been founded, but a small minority have prospered, nor do we think that, as a general rule, the founders of these have been greatly enriched by their prosperity." Only five years after he had extravagantly touted the splendors of Ohiopiomingo, John Nicholson died in debtors' prison, leaving behind a wife and eight children, an army of creditors, and debts amounting to $12 million.

The number of urban failures in the early days of Kentucky and the Ohio Valley may well have exceeded the number of successful townsite promotions, but all of this activity highlights the importance of cities in luring migrants and speculators westward and indicates the extent to which large numbers of people were involved in the city-building process. Pioneer Kentuckians brought with them across the mountains the Puritan conception of cities as bulwarks against the savagery of raw wilderness and as instruments by which civilization could be brought to a vast new land. The urban frontiersmen shared an optimistic and exuberant faith in progress and in the young nation's "untransacted destiny," as well as a confident belief in the power of cities, industry, and technology to speed the transformation of the Ohio Valley from a gloomy wilderness to a flourishing region. Although small by twentieth-century standards, the early cities exerted a disproportionately large influence in the life of the Commonwealth, performing functions and providing services that were historically urban in nature. Even the tiny stockaded outposts that formed the nuclei of infant Louisville and Lexington served as havens for new migrants, shelters in time of attack, centers for religious worship and social gatherings, clearinghouses for economic and commercial activities, and seats of administrative and governmental affairs. As crucibles of culture, nurseries of enterprise, and focal points of scientific and intellectual activity, the towns spearheaded advances in every major area of human endeavor. In so doing they fulfilled the classical role of cities as the agencies of civilization.

By 1815 two societies had emerged in Kentucky, one rural and one urban, with distinct patterns of life, institutions, habits, and modes of thought. A farmer living near Lexington expressed this division in a dialogue between "Rusticus" and "Urbanus" that was printed in the *Kentucky Reporter* in 1811. "Urbanus" scorned the "rude, gross appearance" of his rural neighbor, adding, "how strong you smell of your ploughed ground and corn fields. How dismal, how gloomy your green woods. What a miserable clash your whistling woodland birds are continually making." "Rusticus" responded with the rural stereotype of the city slicker. "What a fine smooth complexion you have, Urbanus: you look like a weed that has grown up in the shade. Can you walk your streets without inhaling the noxious fumes with which your town is pregnant? . . . Can you engage in calm contemplation, when hammers are ringing in every direction—when there is as great a *rattling* as in a storm when the hail descends on our housetops?"

The voyage of the steamboat *Enterprise* on the Ohio and Mississippi rivers in 1815 signaled the beginning of a transportation revolution that fundamentally transformed the economic and urban prospects of Kentucky and the Middle West. By that time the young cities of Louisville and Lexington had achieved a relative degree of urbanity and sophistication that the eastern seaports and the cities of the Old World had reached only after centuries of development. Editor Joseph Charless remembered that on his first trip to the West in 1795 the banks of the Ohio were "a dreary wilderness, the haunt of ruthless savages," while only two decades later he found them "sprinkled with towns" boasting of "spinning and weaving establishments, steam mills, manufactures in various metals, leather, wool, cotton and flax," and "seminaries of learning conducted by excellent teachers." In 1795 Charless and other sojourners still faced hazards on the western waters, and traveled aboard gunwale-enclosed vessels from which artillery and rifle fire were employed to repulse Indian attacks. Two decades later ship companies advertised the scenic attractions of voyages aboard steamboats open on all sides, and the guns once vital for defense now saluted settlements along the way, although larger places quickly banned the practice as "disturbing to the peace." Travelers no longer "discovered" cities in the wilderness, but rather planned their itineraries around visits to Pittsburgh, Cincinnati, Lexington, Louisville, St. Louis, New Orleans, and other thriving communities. Thus by 1815 the roots of an urban civilization had been firmly planted in Kentucky, and the first era in the urban history of the state and the Ohio Valley had drawn to a close.

2

URBAN IMPERIALISM AND RIVALRY

"GAIN! GAIN! GAIN! Gain is the beginning, the middle, and the end, the *alpha* and *omega* of the founders of American towns," English traveler Morris Birkbeck exclaimed in 1817. In the period immediately following the War of 1812 a wave of urban speculation swept Kentucky and the Ohio Valley, set off by the optimism and prosperity of the era, the increasingly cultivated and settled character of the surrounding country, and the fact that a few places like Louisville, Lexington, and Cincinnati had already become populous and thriving cities. The boom was spurred on by an extraordinary currency inflation, widespread credit buying, and the reckless wholesale chartering of banks. "On any spot where a few settlers cluster together," Birkbeck continued, "some enterprising proprietor finds in his selection what he deems a good site for a town; he has it surveyed and laid out in lots, which he sells, or offers for sale by auction. . . . Hundreds of these speculations may have failed but hundreds prosper."

Emphasizing geographical advantages, proximity to established communities, and location astride existing or projected highways of commerce, the promoters of cities in the Commonwealth boldly named their tiny settlements after historic world centers such as Utica, Paris, and Versailles. The "large and beautiful" site once known as "M'Cool's bottom" became the envisioned city of Ghent, Simpson's Ferry was renamed Marion, and two likely prospects were grandiosely denominated Manchester and Savannah. Throughout the state city boosters touted the advantages of places like Elba, thirteen miles from Russellville on the "Wolf Lick fork of Muddy River," Ragarsville, "recently laid off by order of the honorable court of Christian," and Francesburg, "near Highland Creek, Union County, . . . surpassed by no site on the river below Louisville." "Scaevola," writing in Lexington's *Kentucky Reporter* in 1819, claimed that "everywhere within the state has property of this description [town lots] at some time or another within the last few years been pushed up to the most enormous prices justified by no present uses to which it would be applied nor profits which it could yield." Although the panic of 1819 burst the speculative bubble, town booming continued in antebellum Kentucky during succeeding periods of prosperity. In 1835, for example, the proprietors of Midway "on the Railroad" advertised the sale of lots, while twenty years later boosters heralded the advantages of Morganza, located at the junction of three railroads at the mouth of the Big Sandy.

Typically, all of the projected towns were hailed as future great cities. Transylvania, eight miles above Louisville at "the mouth of Harrod's Creek," was "unquestionably the best port on the Ohio" and had the additional albeit dubious advantage of being located "immediately opposite the new town of Utica." The promoters of Dover at "the mouth of Lee's Creek" declared that "a delightful road can be got up the hill leading to Minerva," and confidently proclaimed that aspiring rivals "Calais, which lays just opposite, and Ripley, three miles above, from the narrowness of the river and other disadvantages can never cope with Dover." Palermo, in Union County "immediately opposite the mouth of the Saline," would not only become a thriving commercial emporium but was also "destined to become one of the great places on the whole river for steam works, having an inexhaustible coal mine within half a mile of the river, and the coal not above a foot below the surface." Nature had further blessed it with "one of the richest iron ore banks in the western country." Tiny Shippingport, sandwiched between Louisville and Portland, was touted as "the natural and inevitable port of navigation with New Orleans, Saint Louis and all other places situated on the Mississippi, Missouri, and the tributary streams emptying therein."

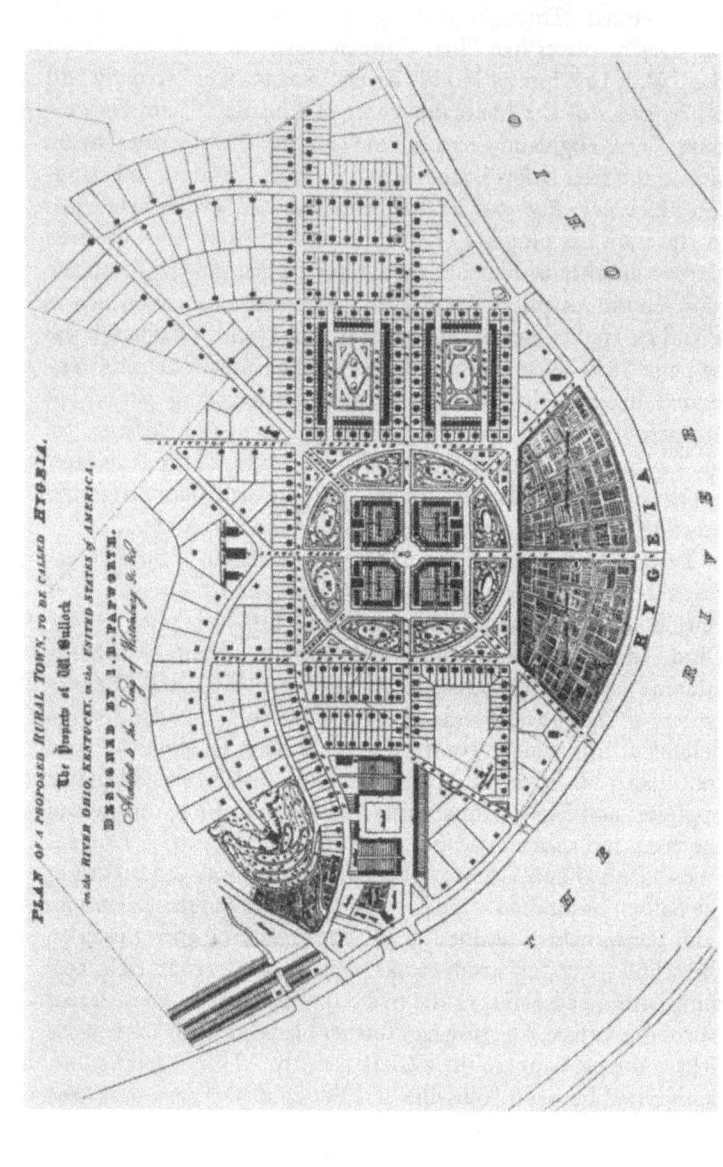

"This was the era of imaginary villages," one observer exclaimed. "Common sense was entirely thrown aside in the calculations of village and city-makers, and impossibilities were deemed feasible of execution." The most elaborately planned Kentucky city during this era was the proposed town of Hygeia, located on the Ohio River opposite Cincinnati. Purchasing a tract of land from a wealthy Kentuckian in 1827, English traveler and lecturer William Bullock planned to build a "town of retirement, in the vicinity of a populous manufacturing city." On his return to England, "determined to have it laid out to the best possible advantage, with professional assistance," Bullock engaged John Buonarotti Papworth, self-proclaimed "Architect to the King of Wirtemburg," as his town planner. An architect of some reputation, Papworth prepared a detailed baroque plan that incorporated most of the forms and building types developed in England during the preceding century. Even though the English traveler Frances Trollope, then living in Cincinnati, praised the "taste and art lavished" on the place, Hygeia soon joined Lystra, Franklinville, and Ohiopiomingo on the growing list of speculative paper towns that never materialized.

By 1830, however, the rise of the city had already become one of the dominant facts of Kentucky and Ohio Valley life. Traveler Simon Ansley O'Ferrall wrote of "towns springing into importance within the memory of comparatively young men," and of log cabins still standing and "shown as the first habitations built by the backwoodsmen, who squatted in the forest where now stand handsome and flourishing cities." Speaking of the entire Ohio Valley, Morgan Neville remarked that "the stranger views here with wonder, the rapidity with which cities sprang up in the forests; and with which barbarism retreats before the approach of art and civilization."

If the achievements of art and civilization nurtured civic pride, the conflicting ambitions of rival cities bred suspicion, jealousy, and vindictiveness, and injected increasing bitterness into interurban affairs. Urban historian Richard C. Wade argued that "one of the most striking characteristics of this period was the development of an urban imperialism which saw rising young giants seek to spread their power and influence over the entire new country. The drive for supremacy . . . was quite conscious, infusing an extraordinary dynamic into city growth, but also breeding bitter rivalries among the claimants." Seeking widespread commercial empires, communities reached out with turnpikes, canals, and railroads to tap far-flung hinterlands. "Like imperial states, cities carved out extensive dependencies, extended their influence over the economic and political life of the hinterland, and fought with contending places over strategic trade routes." The ensuing struggles smashed young villages, smothered promising towns, and even brought down established metropolises.

The most important city in Kentucky to falter was Lexington, dealt a crippling blow by the rise of steamboat traffic on the western rivers. The downward spiral began in 1818 and gathered momentum as the panic of 1819 and the ensuing depression accelerated the pace of the city's decline. Lexington's newspapers increasingly reported bankruptcies, the failure of commercial houses, unemployment, "languishing manufactures," "low prices," "hard times," and "drooping spirits." Property valuations, which had soared from $1,696,249 in 1809 to $3,136,455 in 1816, plummeted thereafter and barely climbed back up to $2 million by 1830. The census of 1820 counted only 5,279 people in Lexington, an increase of but 953 inhabitants over 1810. Louisvillians lost no opportunity to taunt their troubled adversary, and a writer in the *Louisville Correspondent* gloated that "Lexington is, from the concurring reports of all, . . . most deeply shocked throughout all her business, . . . [and is] to Louisville, comparatively in prospect, what Lancaster, Pa. is to Philadelphia." Indeed, by 1830 Lexington, with a population of 6,026, ranked only forty-eighth in size nationally and had fallen behind such places as Taunton, Massachusetts, Alexandria, Virginia, and Lancaster, Pennsylvania. By that time Louisville had surged past her faltering rival, and the once proud "Philadelphia of Kentucky" had been reduced to serving as the commercial center of the Bluegrass region only. A Baltimore traveler who had known Lexington during its golden age was appalled on his return visit to the city in 1829. "I am sorry to say it has degenerated beyond measure," he reported. "The homes and tenants seemed to me to have suffered an equal or similar dilapidation. Where was once the dwelling of gaiety and friendship, with every good and noble sentiment, was now a rusty and moss-grown mansion of ill nature and repulsive indifference." By the mid-1850s Lexington had finally secured its long-sought rail connections with the Ohio River, but this came far too late to enable the city to recapture its position of primacy in the West or even within the Commonwealth. The census of 1860 revealed that Lexington, with a population of 9,321, had fallen to fourth place among the cities of Kentucky.

A number of Lexington's leaders early came to believe that the steamboat so altered all the circumstances of western life that only a radical shift in the town's economy could save it from ruin. They proposed to transform Lexington from a commercial and manufacturing emporium into a cultural mecca, with Transylvania University as the central attraction and magnet. Such a program, a writer in the *Kentucky Reporter* asserted in 1820, "will fill her empty streets, . . . people her tenantless houses, [and] afford a market to her manufactures and [the] produce of that charming and fertile country with which she is surrounded. She will be filled and surrounded with rich men who will patronize the arts, encourage genius and afford a society equal in refinement and intelligence to any of which the world can boast." During the 1820s Lexingtonians consciously adhered to a policy of promoting education and culture in order to reinvigorate their city's crippled economy. This "cultural pump priming," involving municipal, state, and private funds, ultimately proved a poor substitute for genuine economic recovery. But in the short run it provided welcome relief and sustained a number of merchants and landlords who would otherwise have been ruined.

Although the state supplied most of the financial aid to the university, Lexington's municipal government and the city's private citizens were well aware of the institution's economic value and supported it in a variety of ways. In 1820 the city lent the medical division $6,000 for a library and anatomical museum, and gave $500 for a grammar school to be attached to the university. In succeeding years the town council insured Transylvania's buildings for $10,000, endowed a "Lexington Professorship" with $800, and offered $1,300 in scholarships to young men throughout Kentucky. Within five years of his arrival in 1818, Transylvania's President Horace Holley had transformed a small and struggling institution into the highly regarded and influential "Harvard of the West," one of the largest and most prestigious universities in the country. In 1826 the *Kentucky Reporter* declared that "the fact that you cannot find an empty house in Lexington, where in 1818 you may have found many, tells loudly what [the university] has done for the town." By that time a number of academies and girls' schools had grown up around the university, attracting younger students from the state and region; an Atheneum combining a natural history museum with a well-supplied reading room served both scholars and writers; and the city boasted a school of art headed by the well-patronized portraitist Matthew Jouett. Visitors reported that Lexington had definitely "taken on the tone of a literary place," and had become more than ever "the capital of fashion" and "a Paris in miniature" where "a taste for [life's] elegance and luxuries prevails [and where] the fashions and manners of polished Europe are found." Lexington "wears an air of neatness, opulence, and repose, indicating leisure and studiousness, rather than the bustle of business and commerce," Timothy Flint observed in 1832. "There are now much larger towns in the West," he concluded, "but none presenting more beauty and intelligence."

Lexington's cultural renaissance bred jealousy in rival cities, particularly in Cincinnati and Louisville. The editor of the Ohio city's *Liberty Hall* conceded in 1820 that "Cincinnati may be the Tyre, but Lexington is unquestionably the Athens of the West." A desire for total urban supremacy nourished in Cincinnati a gnawing inferiority complex and a seething envy of Lexington's sophistication and polish. One resident maintained that "it may be well for us, when we can catch a moment from the grovelling pursuits of commercial operations, to cull and admire the varied sweets of those literary and scientific effusions, which have stamped Lexington as the headquarters of *Science and Letters* in the Western country." Another Cincinnatian, who believed his city's problem to be more one of public relations, suggested that an ambitious lecture program might "convince those persons at a distance who pronounced us as a *Commercial* people alone, that we have here, both the *Tyre* and the *Athens* of the West." The remarkable success of Transylvania University only heightened Cincinnati's envy, and the editor of the *Western Spy* admitted that it was "particularly mortifying to see the College of a neighboring state attract both Students and Professors" away from home. In the early 1820s Cincinnati established a medical school which it hoped would become "a powerful rival of [Transylvania's college of medicine], and ultimately go beyond it."

During the 1830s Louisville attempted to have Transylvania's medical school moved to the Falls City, alarming and enraging the citizens of Lexington. "No one else," the editor of the *Lexington Intelligencer* fumed on January 30, 1837, "except those who have such a thievish propensity that they can not resist their inclination to appropriate that which belongs to others," could behave as shamelessly as had the denizens of Louisville. Louisville's actions toward Lexington, the *Kentucky Gazette* cried out, were bottomed in "*grasping ambition* and *rapaciousness.*" The following week the editor of the Louisville *Journal* responded to these accusations. "The *Lexington Intelligencer* of Friday speaks of the peculiar 'advantages of a *small* city for the quiet purposes of education and the acquisition of medical science,'" he sneered. "And so the 'modern Athens' really condescends at last to plead her *pigmy size* as a reason why she should maintain the Medical College. We have little doubt, that the reason will, *in her case,* become stronger and stronger every year."

The rivalry between Louisville and Lexington had deep roots and was frequently bitter. Both places had early vied to become the capital of Kentucky. During the early nineteenth century the inland city's dependence on manufacturing created a demand for strong protective tariffs, while the river port's reliance on commerce dictated a policy that favored free trade. By the 1820s Lexington resented Louisville for having acquired much of its former business, while the Falls City coveted Lexington's educational and cultural institutions. When one city helped the other, motives of self-interest could usually be found. The editor of the *Louisville Public Advertiser* supported Lexington's bid for state funds to build a hospital only because he reasoned that if the Bluegrass city obtained such an institution, then "one of the same kind at this place cannot, consistently, be refused." Only the threat of a hostile outsider such as Cincinnati forced the two Kentucky cities to discover their mutual interests and to work together against the common enemy. Thus Lexington supported the Falls City when Cincinnati threatened to build a canal on the Indiana side of the river, while Louisville reciprocated by supporting Transylvania University's request for additional state aid when Cincinnati announced plans to open a competing medical school.

Instances of mutual support were rare, however, and the general tenor of relations between the two communities was acrimonious. Indeed, Louisville far more frequently attacked than came to the aid of Transylvania University, for the school was both the symbol of Lexington's cultural supremacy and the Bluegrass city's most vulnerable institution. "If you wish to jeopardize every amiable trait in the private character of your son, send him to Lexington," the editor of the *Louisville Public Advertiser* warned in 1820, linking the college with political radicalism. "If you wish him to become a Robespierre or a Marat, send him to Lexington to learn the rudiments of Jacobinism and disorganization." Nine years later the newspaper was still hammering away at the school's reputation, cautioning parents that at Transylvania their children would be "surrounded by political desperadoes" and that "the very atmosphere of the place has been calculated to pollute the morals and principles of the youth attending it." Lexingtonians were stunned by the ferocity of the attack, believing that of all their institutions, Transylvania "was the pride and boast of the town" and the one "least calculated to excite the envy and stir up the opposition of any individual or section of the country." They defended their university by detailing its achievements, publicizing testimonials written by graduates and local citizens, and extolling Transylvania's positive influence on students and its role in improving the healthfulness and the "literary atmosphere" of the new country. But by the late 1820s the institution's administrators and trustees had alienated Jacksonian Democrats, farmers, and conservative religious forces, thereby rendering Transylvania's already weakened position all but untenable. President Holley's resignation, chronic financial problems, and a calamitous fire brought about the end of the university's golden age and completed the destruction Louisvillians had long sought of their rival's most substantial economic prop. Ironically, the Falls City had thus helped pave the way for equally hated rival Cincinnati to emerge as both the "Athens" and the "Tyre" of the West.

The steamboat that had spelled Lexington's decline also signaled Louisville's ascendance. By slashing distances and travel time, steam navigation transformed the Ohio Valley into a settled and cultivated region in a single generation. A northward and eastward movement of goods came to supplement downriver commerce, as steamboats and a series of canals constructed in the 1820s and 1830s connected the Ohio Valley to the Great Lakes and to the Atlantic seaboard. British observer Henry Bradshaw Fearon noted in 1817 that Louisville was "daily becoming a most important town, being the connecting link between New Orleans and the whole western country," while Falls City printer Richard W. Otis likened the steamboat to "an enchanted rod waved over progress." The city's population more than doubled during the 1820s, jumping from 4,012 to 10,341, and in 1823 Italian visitor J.C. Beltrami proclaimed that "if Pittsburgh be the Tyre, and Cincinnati the Carthage of the Ohio, Louisville is its Syracuse." Commerce remained the heart of the city's economy and the mainspring of its growth. By 1830 Louisville had become the center of steamboat operations on the Ohio, handling the bulk of the immense tonnage that moved over the river. "The gun of the arriving or departing steamboats is heard at every hour of the day and the night," Timothy Flint asserted in 1828, "and no person has an adequate idea of the business and bustle of Louisville, until he has arrived at the town." In 1836 Gabriel Collins, employing the geographical determinism typical of urban promotion during this period, proclaimed in his city directory that "Louisville is as clearly marked out by nature, as the great heart of western commerce, as New Orleans is, as the great mart of the South."

By the 1830s Louisville had begun to fulfill the dreams of its early prophets, assuming the characteristics of a prosperous regional metropolis. "Main Street, for the distance of about one mile, presents a proud display of wealth and grandeur," visitor Caleb Atwater wrote in 1831. "The stores, filled with the commodities and manufactures of every clime, and every art, dazzle the eye, [and] the ringing of the bells and the roaring of the guns

View of Main Street, Louisville, circa 1835

View of the public landing at Louisville, 1856

belonging to the numerous steamboats in the harbor, the cracking of the coachman's whip, and the sound of the stage driver's horn, salute the ear." Between 1830 and 1860 Louisville strengthened its commercial position and remained the largest urban center on the Ohio River below Cincinnati. During the 1840s manufacturing began to increase in importance, and by the eve of the Civil War Louisville had become the twelfth largest manufacturing center in the country and the largest industrial center in the South. Louisville "has grown withall at a Western rapidity," traveler Frederick Law Olmsted reported in 1857, having "great business, both as an entrepôt and as itself, a manufacturing producer." Although lacking the charm of New Orleans or the "whirr" of Cincinnati, the Falls City represented "a good specimen of a brisk and well-furnished city."

The dramatic increase in the volume of trade on the western rivers following the introduction of the steamboat sharpened the already bitter commercial rivalry between Louisville and Cincinnati. From the earliest days of settlement, Cincinnatians envisioned and conspired to build some kind of canal at the Falls of the Ohio that would facilitate the flow of commerce on the river. During the opening decades of the nineteenth century, Cincinnati—described as a "hot bed of projects"—supported various schemes to build a canal at the falls, usually on the Indiana side of the river. Louisville residents fought these efforts at every turn, fearing that a canal would eliminate the transshipment business and perhaps destroy their city's economic foundations. They attempted to counter every Cincinnati initiative by promoting rival canal plans of their own, suggesting alternative projects such as improved roads around the falls, mounting propaganda campaigns, and devising ingenious delaying tactics. Queen City spokesmen depicted Louisville as "a little town" that was trying to keep "all the upper country tributary to it" by compelling merchants to deposit their goods in its warehouses and to pay extravagant prices for transportation around the falls.

Cincinnati, anxious both to loosen commerce on the Ohio and to weaken its economic rival, had a deep stake in a canal at the falls. "No question was ever agitated here that involved more important consequences to this town," the editor of *Liberty Hall* announced in 1817. The newspaper lent its support to the Jeffersonville Ohio Canal Company, chartered in 1817 by the Indiana legislature, and assured potential investors that "the wealth, influence, enterprise and talents of Cincinnati are at the head of this measure." If Queen City residents failed to support the project, the editor warned, they "deserved to be hewers of wood and drawers of water" for Louisville. Cincinnatians responded by contributing funds, providing more than half the company's directors, and sending one of their most prominent spokesmen to give the ceremonial address as digging began. "If the obstruction continues," the editor of the *Cincinnati Advertiser* cautioned in 1818, "Louisville will be the place of deposit, and will undoubtedly become rich and populous; but it will be at the expense of all the country above it. The prosperity of Cincinnati, which has increased in wealth and population beyond example, will be checked; its capital transferred to Louisville; its population diverted to the same place." Thus, he concluded, "the increasing importance of a canal round the Falls of the Ohio, is rendered more evident by every day's experience."

Residents of the Queen City found it difficult to believe that anyone in Louisville could truly support a canal. "The future growth of [the Falls City] depends upon the obstruction," the editor of *Liberty Hall* declared in 1818; "remove it and Louisville dwindles into insignificance; the very unwholesomeness of its atmosphere, after the stir of business had subsided, would make it a deserted village." The *Cincinnati Advertiser* charged that "it is the people *above the falls,* whose interest it is to cut a canal, and it is vain and absurd for them to expect assistance from those whose interests are diametrically opposed." The *Western Spy* concurred, predicting that if Louisville built the channel it would be "of no real advantage to the country above the falls; for Louisville can afford . . . several hundred thousand dollars, to construct an *inefficient* canal, if by that means a removal of the obstacles in the river could be prevented; which, if they remain, are worth millions to that town."

The editor of the *Louisville Public Advertiser* responded to these charges by branding Cincinnatians a suspicious, greedy, calculating lot. "The people of Cincinnati, if they are like their journalists, cannot believe, that those of Louisville will assist in opening a canal, for the same reason that a miser always despairs of being befriended by his neighbor," he self-righteously proclaimed. "He is incapable of experiencing a single manly or generous emotion of the heart, and his despicable selfishness leads him to suppose, the balance of mankind are influenced by the same detestable causes." The *Western Spy* simply repeated its charges and asserted that the Falls City's days of prosperity were numbered. "If Louisville really is a small town now, with the profits of trade of the Upper Ohio flowing into her hands, what must she become when the route of this trade shall be changed? Will not her epitaph be written?"

The increase in river traffic stimulated by the steamboat intensified the feelings of envy and bitterness in the contending cities. "I discovered two ruling passions in Cincinnati," a visitor claimed in 1819; "enmity against Pittsburgh and jealousy of Louisville." The editor of Cincinnati's *Western Spy* ridiculed the suggestion that the Queen City might be jealous of her smaller downstream rival. "Louisville is little else than a place of deposit; Cincinnati is a great commercial city, with an immense extent of country, rich, well watered, and thickly inhabited, depending on it both for a market and supply," he trumpeted. "Louisville rises from the bosom of an extensive marsh, whose pestiferous exhalations sicken and destroy one third of its inhabitants yearly; Cincinnati on her hills is the abode of health herself. The importance of Louisville sinks when the route of transportation is changed; Cincinnati would have grown in strength and grandeur had such a place as Louisville never existed. Look at the age, and present condition of the two places. In fine, Cincinnati is the emporium of all territory northwest of the Ohio; Louisville is a small trading town at the Falls of the Ohio River, which is now struggling to avoid a dissolution which is foreseen. . . . Jealousy of Louisville could have never entered the mind of any thinking man in Cincinnati. If such a mean passion exists, it must be found in Louisville towards Cincinnati."

Jeffersonville, Indiana, tied its own metropolitan ambitions to those of the Queen City, and bitterly resented Louisville's attempts to sabotage a canal on the northern shore of the Ohio River above the falls. "Louisville with all her display is a town to let," the Jeffersonville *Indianian* charged in 1819, "and if exposed to public auction and the whole world for bidders, would not fetch enough to pay the debts of its inhabitants." The editor of the *Louisville Public Advertiser* replied that "it is better to have a town for let than no town at all," and dismissed the Jeffersonville Canal as a "contemptible ditch, which a respectable Dutch farmer would not consider a respectable mill-race." The irate editor of the *Indianian* retorted that his counterpart on the *Public Advertiser* had become diseased with "sub phobia *canalis villae Jeffersoniensis.*"

Louisvillians reluctantly came to support a canal in order to prevent their rivals from building a channel on the Indiana side of the river. In 1825 Kentucky incorporated the Louisville and Portland Canal Company, which after many delays finally completed its work in 1833. Despite fears of diminished commercial importance, Louisville actually flourished as never before, as the volume and the value of commerce on the Ohio grew during the 1830s and 1840s. Even the transshipment business rebounded after an initial setback, as the much larger steamboats constructed after 1830 simply could not negotiate locks designed to handle the smaller vessels of an earlier era. Indeed, frustrated merchants in rival cities began calling for the enlargement of the canal almost from the day it opened, but new construction would not begin until 1860 and would then take a dozen years to complete.

As the commercial rivalry between Louisville and Cincinnati provided the backdrop against which the Louisville and Portland Canal was built, so the economic struggle between Louisville and Nashville set the stage for the construction of the Louisville and Nashville Railroad. Each community saw the railroad as a major weapon in its campaign to achieve commercial dominance over the other as well as over regional competitors such as Cincinnati, Chattanooga, Atlanta, Mobile, and New Orleans. During dry seasons of the year the Falls City found itself challenged by Nashville, located at the head of navigation on the Cumberland River, as a distributing center for the border region, and also found itself cut off from outside sources of coal and other essential supplies. A railroad to the South would enable Louisville to break through its commercial isolation when the Ohio was impassable, to neutralize rival Nashville, and to gain the jump on Cincinnati in the quest for southern markets. Ambitious Nashville interests supported railroads in order to end their city's dependence on the river, to capture southern markets, and to build their community into the great distributing center of the South.

A serious challenge from Nashville in the late 1840s prompted Louisville entrepreneurs to revive railroad schemes that had been temporarily abandoned following the economic panic of 1837. When the Tennessee capital, with encouragement from the Kentucky communities of Bowling Green and Glasgow, threatened to build a railroad far enough north to penetrate Louisville's markets but without actually entering the city, Falls City interests were roused to action. Fearing that Louisville might become effectively isolated between Cincinnati and Nashville, citizens attending a mass meeting in early 1850 adopted a resolution offering to subscribe $1 million of city funds in a railroad to run from Louisville to the South. The following year the Louisville General Council approved a subscription for that amount, which enabled the city to name seven directors to the board of the newly chartered Louisville and Nashville Railroad, and later in the decade the city subscribed another $825,000 to the company. The L&N would both thwart Nashville's projected railway into Kentucky and enable Louisville merchants and manufacturers to tap Nashville's rail line to Atlanta. The decision of Louisville's business leaders to strike out toward Memphis from the main stem of the L&N at Bowling Green would also enable the Falls City to siphon off some of the Mississippi River trade at the Tennessee emporium. The Louisville and Nashville Railroad, completed to Nashville in 1859 and to Memphis the following year, established Louisville as the "Gateway to the South" and provided the best channel of trade between the Ohio Valley and the South until the completion of the Cincinnati Southern Railroad nearly twenty years later.

In January 1856 a writer in the *Commercial Review*, the organ of the Louisville Chamber of Commerce, argued that railroads had "already become our great channels of trade and travel, throwing canals completely in the shade and rendering rivers, so far as human movements are concerned, of secondary importance." So influential was the railroad considered that in 1855 the city council altered Louisville's official seal from "a representation of a wharf with boxes and bales thereon [and] a steamboat approaching the wharf" to a depiction of "a locomotive under way" with the motto "Progress."

At mid-century, "progress" seemed a most appropriate motto for the burgeoning city at the Falls of the Ohio. The community's population had risen steadily from 10,341 in 1830 to 21,210 in 1840 to 43,194 in 1850, and Louisville had moved up in rank from seventeenth to eleventh to tenth largest city in the country. In a promotional work published in 1852, Ben Casseday lyrically proclaimed Louisville's prospects in a style and manner reminiscent of Connolly and Campbell's 1774 advertisement. "Here is a space of level country beyond the reach of any flood, all parts of which are equally well adapted to the purposes of the builder, sufficiently large to contain within its limits the cities of London, Paris, and St. Petersburg, with the foundation for a large city already laid, with a location which, in reference to facilities of intercourse with the rest of the United States, is unsurpassed; at the only point of obstruction in a continuous line of two thousand miles of inland navigation; a half-way house between North and South; a point through which all the great railroad arteries must of necessity pass; in the center of the most fertile and productive agricultural lands in the Union. . . . What is there, in view of all these circumstances, to prevent it from becoming the Great City of the West?"

Large-scale forces were already at work, however, that would soon shatter Louisville's dreams. During the 1840s St. Louis took its place as the commercial metropolis of the rapidly expanding upper Middle West, while Cincinnati appropriated the lion's share of the mounting commerce of the Ohio Valley and became the nexus of trade lines stretching from the Atlantic Ocean to the Gulf of Mexico. During the following decade, moreover, the long-range prospects of all of the river cities were diminished as several trunk railroad lines connected the Atlantic seaports with the Ohio and Mississippi valleys, reinforcing the shift of the main axis of trade away from a predominantly north-south orientation on the rivers toward an east-west flow along canals and railways.

By the eve of the Civil War Cincinnati had emerged as the reigning metropolis of the Ohio Valley and the sixth largest city in the nation, with a population of 161,044. Although Louisville's population had climbed to 68,033 by 1860, the Falls City had dropped a notch from tenth to eleventh rank in size, marking the onset of a prolonged slide. "To all intents and purposes [Louisville] is a completely finished city, evidently presenting no change," a Cincinnati editor gloated. "There appears to be some stir of business on Main Street which serves to relieve the otherwise dull monotony of the place. A walk of one square from this street, in any direction, places you in comparative retirement."

At times during the antebellum decades Cincinnati's expansion program had threatened almost all of the cities in the Commonwealth, forcing them to band together to try to stymie the imperial ambitions of the Ohio metropolis. In 1835 Cincinnati promoter Daniel Drake spearheaded a drive to investigate "the practicality and advantage" of constructing a $7 million railroad between the Queen City and Charleston, South Carolina, described by the *American Rail-Road Journal and Advocate of Internal Improvements* as "the noblest work of inland communication ever projected." Kentucky, with its mighty river system, seemed to have little to gain, and as the editor of the *Maysville Eagle* declared, "it would by no means become our State to contribute to the prosperity of the rival city, by allowing the road to pass through our territory." Only Covington, situated directly across the Ohio River from Cincinnati, viewed the railway as a means of furthering its own plans for growth and approved the original proposal. Louisville, Lexington, Maysville, and Frankfort all believed the Cincinnati project endangered their own urban aspirations, and when the Kentucky legislature debated granting a charter to the railroad in January 1836, they suggested alternative northern termini within the Commonwealth. "It was properly made to appear to be an effort on the part of the cities of Charleston and Cincinnati, to divert trade from the channel which God and Nature had prepared," the *Eagle*'s editor asserted. The bill would cause "the ruin and destruction of the cities, towns, and the capitalists situated on those great waters" of the Ohio and Mississippi unless the legislature protected them. "The cities of Kentucky are struggling for self-preservation; Cincinnati through her friends in the Kentucky Legislature, is out to engross the entire commerce of Kentucky, establish and perpetuate her supremacy, and, as a necessary consequence, ensure the prostration of the commercial interests of the cities." A compromise was finally reached by which branch lines would run to Louisville and Maysville, and the company was officially organized in January 1837 as the Louisville, Cincinnati & Charleston Railroad. Attempts to recharter the railroad to provide banking privileges produced renewed tension, and South Carolina's Governor George McDuffie complained that the corporation had been "required to construct two branches, making together 150 miles of rail road, obviously against their own interest, and merely to *accommodate two towns in Kentucky.*" The editor of the *Louisville Public Advertiser* replied straightforwardly that "Kentucky was unwilling to destroy her own towns." Had Kentucky given its assent to the original plan, he continued, "Cincinnati would have been made the New York of the Ohio Valley." The Louisville newspaper continued its efforts to defeat the bill, the new charter failed by six votes, and the economic depression which followed the panic of 1837 along with other circumstances finally killed the project in 1839.

The proposed railroad from Cincinnati to Charleston sharpened the urban rivalry between Louisville and Covington. Although Covington defended itself as "no contemptible rival of Cincinnati," the editor of the *Louisville Public Advertiser* reflected the opinion of most Kentuckians when in 1837 he branded the community a mere pawn of the Queen City. Dismissing Covington as "one of the suburbs of Cincinnati," he relegated the town along with nearby Newport to the status of subversive and submissive satellites betraying their homeland in the interests of a foreign power. "Covington is overshadowed by Cincinnati, and so she must remain," the editor charged. "Competition between the two places is out of the question; and we think it is unreasonable to urge Kentucky to sacrifice her principal towns in order to give Covington an opportunity to assist augmenting the commerce and wealth and influence of Cincinnati. . . . The 'engulphing city' of which the [Covington] *North Kentuckian* should complain, is Cincinnati. That place controls and partly owns Newport and

Covington. It has literally colonized [the two towns], . . . and makes them battle for her in the Legislative Halls of Kentucky. . . . We are sorry Newport and Covington cannot become important points."

The furious editor of the *North Kentuckian* responded by branding the Falls City a greedy, voracious, unscrupulous adversary. "The rank, unmitigated selfishness of her policy, her unjust, aye, and unwise attempt to check every improvement which does not directly throw treasure into her lap, to prevent any other portion of the state from acquiring new advantages, and even to filch those it may already possess, are characteristics it were well for the people to understand." The editor of the *Public Advertiser* replied that some Covingtonians "might be materially edified by reading the story of the fly perched on the coach wheel, exclaiming as the vehicle drove onward, 'Gods! what a dust I make.' . . . Covington is not selfish, not she. It would be cruel to charge her with 'selfishness,' when she is so zealously laboring to remove Lexington to Cincinnati; to draw half the trade of Cincinnati to her. . . . An infant *City* that would make sacrifices so large, for a prospective return so small, must be pronounced *extremely liberal.*"

By 1860 Covington and Newport had become the second and third largest cities in Kentucky, with 16,471 and 10,046 inhabitants, respectively, yet they remained extensions of Cincinnati. Traveler John Melish early observed that Newport was "a small place . . . quite eclipsed by the splendour of Cincinnati," while visitor George Ogden noticed that the streets of Covington were "laid out as to appear as a continuation of those of Cincinnati." Other visitors echoed Ogden's observation and included Newport as well. "The streets of these towns," John Woods wrote in 1822, "are laid out to correspond with those of Cincinnati, so that from the upper part of the city you see the streets of Newport and Covington, without perceiving the river between them, and thus the whole appears but one town." Covington and Newport were more closely bound to Cincinnati than were New Albany and Jeffersonville to Louisville, but all of these smaller communities grew up in the shadows of their cross-river metropolitan neighbors and became economic appendages of them.

Conflicting urban aspirations also exacerbated tensions between Louisville and her Ohio falls neighbor New Albany, Indiana's largest city until the mid-1850s. Eager to tap the rapidly expanding market to the north, Louisville entrepreneurs decided in 1836 to construct a bridge across the Ohio to link up with Indiana's proposed railroads. "The stock is taken; the funds are ready," the editor of the *Louisville Journal* announced; "so that our goodly sister New Albany, if she has any objection to living hereafter in close proximity with Louisville, and reposing under the generous shadow of her outstretched wing, cannot pack up and be off down the river or into the interior a moment too soon." The outraged editor of the *New-Albany Gazette* quickly responded to Louisville's proffered shelter. "We are saluted with the *'generous shadow of the outstretched wing of Louisville,'*" he thundered. "Rather a Upas poison, or Anaconda embrace, devouring everything it can feed upon. . . . We think the fishes of the Falls may rest assured that they are to have yet many years of sweet repose before they will be disturbed in their watery beds by this great 'enterprise,' crossing the river." (The fishes would indeed enjoy their "sweet repose" for more than another thirty years.) Louisville continued to covet the trade centered at New Albany, and the editor of the *Louisville Democrat* advised in 1850 that "a plank road to some suitable point below the Falls, would, without doubt, bring to Louisville the trade of a large extent of country on the Indiana side, which, for the want of this facility and transportation, is now centered in New Albany." Louisville businessmen also prepared plans for a railway between their city and Portland as well as for a new wharf below Portland at a point more nearly opposite New Albany. These projects would enable Kentucky merchants and shippers "to reap the full advantage of the enterprise that is constructing a railroad from New Albany through some of the richest portions of Indiana up to the lakes," as the *Louisville Journal* suggested. The editor of the *New Albany Daily Ledger* complained that the plan for a new wharf at "West Louisville . . . exhibits plainly the designs of Louisville upon the legitimate business of New Albany—business which it has cost them, individually and collectively, much of their means and efforts to secure. . . . It shows that no exertion will be spared by Louisville to secure to herself the fruits of our labor and enterprise, to which she has no more claim or right than has a town in the island of Japan."

The fate of youthful communities in Kentucky often hinged on timely action and aggressive entrepreneurship. When the Louisville and Nashville Railroad was chartered in 1850, every hamlet between the two terminal cities viewed the project as a potential vehicle for its own urban ambitions. There ensued a mad scramble among these places to try to persuade the new company to run its tracks through their respective towns. There were two alternative routes through Kentucky, the lower route which would pass through Elizabethtown, Bowling Green, and Franklin, and the upper or "air-line" route which would pass through Bardstown, Glasgow, Scottsville, and New Haven. In September 1851 the L&N's board shrewdly passed a resolution stating that it had no preference as to route and that local subscription pledges should decide the matter. Proponents of both routes began a bidding war, and the dispute crystallized around the conflicting ambitions of Bowling Green on the lower route and Glasgow on the upper. Glasgow moved slowly and eventually offered $300,000. But Bowling Green took decisive action. Recognizing that a railroad would be the key to their city's aspirations, Bowling Green entrepreneurs refused to play the L&N's waiting game. They procured a charter similar to the L&N's from the Tennessee legislature in February 1852 and announced their intention of building their *own* railroad from Bowling Green to Nashville. The company promptly put surveyors in the field and opened subscription books, while the citizens of the city approved a subscription of $1 million to the company's stock. The board of the L&N could no longer ignore the threat of a competing line, and in May 1852 it authorized a consolidation of the two companies. Although the lower route offered fewer serious engineering problems, passed through some large coal beds, and could easily be linked to Memphis, Bowling Green's bold and independent action played a major role in the ultimate decision to follow the lower route. The different responses of Bowling Green and Glasgow to the same challenge helped shape the destinies of both places.

By 1860 more than 120,000 people, or slightly over 10 percent of Kentucky's total population, lived in the eight urban places in the state having 2,500 people or more. In 1840 towns and cities were still concentrated in the inner Bluegrass region, along the Ohio River, and between the inner Bluegrass and Louisville. Only two decades later urbanization had begun to transform all but the southeastern and south-central portions of the Commonwealth. Although the Bluegrass centers still predominated, cities were rising from Ashland and Catlettsburg in the east where the Big Sandy joins the Ohio, to Columbus and Hickman in the far west on the Mississippi River. In between, places like Maysville, Newport, Covington, Carrollton, Louisville, Owensboro, Henderson, and Paducah thrived on the trade carried along the Ohio River, while other communities emerged along Kentucky's principal tributary rivers. In the west-central portion of the state away from the Ohio and Mississippi, places like Russellville, Hopkinsville, Bowling Green, Franklin, and Madisonville had begun to grow. Paducah had attained a population of 4,590, Frankfort had reached 3,702, and Owensboro and Hopkinsville had climbed to 2,308 and 2,289, respectively.

By 1860 a half-century of vigorous urban imperialism and rivalry had established the outlines of the emerging urban network in Kentucky. Urban ambitions had given rise to a haphazard transportation matrix comprised of turnpikes, canals, and railroads, which connected the sections of the Commonwealth, provided access to distant markets, and formed one of the cornerstones of a developing regional economy. The hunger for power and primacy, the fear of failure, and the constant search for new markets drove aspiring communities to provide the funds and leadership for, to determine the routes of, and generally to reap the largest rewards from the transportation revolution. When the Louisville and Nashville Railroad was completed in 1859, the celebration held in the Falls City was described as "the greatest occasion in the Annals of the West." A "*feu de joie* of champagne corks kept rattling like hail on a sky-light," and proud Louisvillians confidently maintained that their city was destined to become "the very center of a vast network of [rail]roads." As urban historians Charles N. Glaab and A. Theodore Brown pointed out, "town rivalry was one of the great games of nineteenth-century America. . . . [The] urban rallying cry, . . . heard through the land at every promising spot on road and river, . . . reflect[ed] the creating of magnificent cities in the wilderness through hope, enthusiasm, and energy." Urban imperialism provided an incalculable stimulus to commercial and industrial enterprise, and success bred a strong pride in community accomplishment.

Defeat in an urban rivalry, however, bred bitterness, jealousy, and resentment. Early in its history Portland, at the lower end of the Falls of the Ohio, had ambitions to become a large place, and Henry McMurtrie predicted in 1819 that "its future destinies may be considered as those of a highly flourishing and important town." But in 1852 Portland was annexed by the city of Louisville, and Ben Casseday reported in that year that "it has never equalled the least sanguine hopes of its friends [and] has no history of its own worthy of relation." On the evening of December 13, 1860, residents of the former town of Portland met at Fred Duckwall's saloon and voted to reestablish their independence as the "Confederacy of Portland." The headline of the *Courier* on the fifteenth screamed: "AWFUL! TERRIBLE! GRAND! GLOOMY! AND PECULIAR! PORTLAND SECEDED!!" The delegates resolved "that all drivers of drays, hacks, baggage and express wagons, and other vehicles of transport and travel, . . . pay such a per cent of duty before entering the port as will enable the Confederacy of Portland to be perfectly independent of all nations of the world." In other resolutions the citizens of "glorious old Portland" proclaimed that "the lower end of the Louisville and Portland Canal where the tolls are collected belongs to us," laid claim to public buildings and property throughout the city of Louisville, stated that "we do not care whether Shippingport joins us or not," and adopted their own flag displaying "two Catfish, *saltant*, on a market stall for a background." Behind this jest lay a still smoldering resentment the residents of Portland felt toward the metropolis that had devoured their town, a resentment not dissimilar to the antipathy agrarian southerners harbored toward what they perceived to be a rapacious, imperialistic, urban North. Neither for Portland nor for the South was a self-proclaimed confederacy destined to become "perfectly independent of all nations of the world."

3

THE FIRST URBAN CRISIS

During the early decades of the nineteenth century, the cities in the Commonwealth were challenged by an urban crisis of formidable proportions and frustrating complexity. As young communities with little knowledge of the workings of municipal government, they had to struggle to meet the basic needs of rapidly expanding populations with inadequate revenues and with antiquated customs derived from rural and village experiences. Urbanization overwhelmed municipal administrations in Kentucky as elsewhere, and across the country civic leaders turned in desperation to temporary expedients, haphazard methods, and stopgap measures. "In nearly every field of municipal authority—police, fire, streets, water, and health—conditions deteriorated so rapidly that a series of emergencies appeared, requiring decisive action," historian Richard C. Wade argued. "Any one of these was grave enough to tax the ingenuity of local authorities, yet the crises came on many fronts. Indeed, the multiplicity of issues was the real danger. Communities could handle some of the challenges, but not all. Yet their interrelatedness made success in any single one difficult." Confronting an unprecedented array of problems during this era, city governments moved haltingly yet progressively to define and provide a range of urban services.

Those Kentucky cities that had attained substantial populations by 1860 had done so almost overnight. Louisville's population more than doubled during every decade between 1800 and 1850, mushrooming from a mere 500 or so up to nearly 45,000. Newport and Covington grew from tiny hamlets of 715 and 743 inhabitants in 1830 into burgeoning cities of 10,046 and 16,471, respectively, in 1860. During the same thirty-year period Owensboro's population increased from 229 to 2,308, while Paducah's jumped from 105 to 4,590.

Rapid population growth led to increasing congestion, haphazard construction, the filling in of vacant and rear lots, and the selling off of remaining public lands. As once picturesque vistas of countryside and rivers disappeared behind warehouses, factories, and shops, residents and visitors alike bemoaned the absence of thoughtful urban planning and orderly development. As early as 1797 traveler Moses Austin complained that "Louis Ville by nature is beautiful but the handy work of Man has instead of improving destroyed the works of Nature and made it a detestable place." Henry McMurtrie lamented the despoiling of the Falls City's riverfront and criticized early residents for their "flagrant want of taste. . . . Had the first, or Main street, been laid off so as to have extended 90 feet from the brink of the second bank, forming an avenue [in] front of the town, and had no houses been permitted to exist north of that avenue . . . Louisville would have exhibited a *coup d'oeil*, surpassed, in point of beauty, by few in the world. As it is, the town has turned its back upon the varied and interesting prospect presented by the Ohio and its Falls."

The pressure of increasing population also led to the beginnings of suburban growth. As early as 1832 the proprietor of Woodland Garden, adjacent to the Butchertown section of Louisville, promoted his community as "not only THE NEAREST RETREAT FROM THE CITY, but . . . the most extensive; affording many acres of land under high cultivation, *Groves of native trees* and a GARDEN abounding in all the necessaries and luxuries of life." Tensions and conflicts between cities and their suburbs emerged early. Lexington's assessor complained in 1813 that residents in the out-lots "alleged no benefit resulted to them from either the Watch, Lamps, fire buckets or fire companies," and hence refused to pay their taxes. Louisvillians charged that residents of Shippingport and Portland enjoyed municipal services without paying for them, and in the late 1820s the Falls City launched a movement to incorporate the two communities in order to widen its tax base.

As the cities grew, tensions between urban and rural interests increased and became a major factor in political and legislative affairs. In local and regional elections, even though rural inhabitants easily outnumbered urbanites, the city dwellers were able to wield disproportionate power by virtue of their better organization and leadership. During the 1820s, for example, residents of Louisville cast but one-fourth of a combined total of 3,200 votes in Jefferson and Oldham counties, yet the state senator and both representatives came from the city. When a third assemblyman was added in 1829, rural interests pleaded with Louisville leaders to name someone from outside the city. One observer wrote in the *Louisville Public Advertiser* that "it may seem strange that it would be necessary thus to ask for the liberality of 800 voters, in favor of 2,400. . . . Nevertheless, the concentrated energies of 800 do entirely outweigh the scattered influence of the 2,400—that all past experience teaches." The cities were keen to have representatives in Frankfort who would be "warmly attached" to urban interests. When there was an attempt in 1828 to pass a reapportionment bill that would have gerrymandered Kentucky's assembly districts to the detriment of the cities, the editor of the *Louisville Public Advertiser* charged that the sole object of the measure was "to curtail the weight and influence of both town [Louisville] and county [Jefferson] in the councils of the state."

Although cities could dominate their immediate regions, rural interests early gained control of the state legislature and the "councils of the state." The rural-dominated legislature parceled out privileges to the cities reluctantly and by dribs and drabs, responding to petitions for incorporation with specific grants of meager privileges in charters that narrowly defined the limits of town authority and failed to allow for urban expansion. Louisville's and Lexington's first rights extended merely over land, and as the cities grew, problems arose which necessitated additional legislation and almost constant charter revision. Louisville's basic document had to be amended twenty-two times before 1815, as the Kentucky legislature needed to be convinced year after year that, as it admitted in 1808, "the several laws heretofore passed relative to the town of Louisville, are inadequate to the purposes intended." State authorities did, however, rapidly grant municipalities the responsibility for providing basic urban services such as the paving, cleaning, and repairing of streets, fire and police protection, the provision of water and lighting, the regulation of markets, and the removal of nuisances.

But the legislature hamstrung local authorities by including in all charters stringent limitations on taxation. Denied the power to tax freely, Kentucky cities continually pleaded with state authorities to increase their allowances. "Are we to be constantly running down to Frankfort—pray give us 1000 dollars, this year—500 more the year after—and 100 more the next?" the exasperated editor of Lexington's *Kentucky Reporter* asked in 1810. The legislature increased Louisville's maximum assessment from the original £25 to $200 in 1803, $800 in 1805, and $2,000 in 1812, but the rate never surpassed 1 percent of real and personal property. The cities turned to other sources of revenue, such as rent from market stalls, wagon and cart fees, tavern licenses, and court fines, but these never amounted to more than one-fourth of the whole income. When local governments resorted to financing improvements by borrowing, either from private banks or by issuing their own notes, the state responded by enacting debt-limitation legislation.

During their formative decades, therefore, Kentucky cities had barely enough revenue to provide the essential urban services they were given responsibility for, let alone sufficient funds to meet emergency needs. "The proceeds of seven years taxes," the trustees of Lexington argued in 1796, "will be insufficient to build stone bridges, and to make sewers for carrying off water, to sink wells and erect pumps . . . and to make such other repairs, as are necessary for the health, safety and convenience of their fellow citizens." Two decades later the trustees of Louisville declared that their income was "entirely insufficient to answer the purposes of the town." Towns petitioned to become cities in part to secure the increased fiscal responsibility and more substantial home rule embodied in city charters in provisions for greater revenue, loosened debt restrictions, and broadened enforcement powers. In 1828, when Louisville became a city, the annual budget climbed to $40,000, and the following year a special committee reported that "the finances of the city are favorable to a vigorous prosecution of the system of improvements by the extending of the graduation and paving of the streets, filling & draining of the ponds," and other programs.

Yet neither Louisville nor any other city in the state enjoyed sufficient revenue to enable it to provide a full range of urban services. Priorities had to be established, programs carefully chosen, and some projects delayed indefinitely. That the wealthiest merchants dominated the city councils and boards of trustees guaranteed that mercantile considerations would govern the allocation of scarce resources. Projects deemed essential for the growth of trade, such as market facilities, wharves, and improved streets, were generally given preference over the provision of schools, drainage of stagnant pools of water, and establishment of an effective watch. In 1819 McMurtrie accused Louisville's trustees of allowing police protection to deteriorate while they concentrated on commercial issues, and warned that "as long as the trustees or other officers are chosen from among mercantile men . . . so long will the town have to take care of itself."

Because commercial enterprise depended on the ability to move men and merchandise rapidly into and through the towns, the primary concern of the young communities became the paving of main arteries and central thoroughfares. Indeed, the quest for adequate all-weather streets occasioned more legislation and consumed more revenue than any other single issue. Trustees frequently devoted entire meetings to grading and paving, and budgets regularly allocated between one-fourth and one-half of all disbursements to these projects. In 1811, for example, Lexington spent $1,790 out of a total budget of $4,300 on street improvement and repair, while in 1830 Louisville allocated $17,031 out of $46,245 for surfacing and cleaning.

Despite such large expenditures, most streets and thoroughfares in and around Kentucky's cities remained unimproved and unpaved, dusty in good weather and muddy in bad. A resident of the Falls City declared in 1822 that "there is not a worse mud-hole within 20 miles of Louisville, than our much admired MAIN

STREET." He estimated that the "unwary traveller" would need an escort of four policemen in order to "circumnavigate that 'Slough of Despond.'" Mrs. Basil Hall, visiting Louisville in 1828, reported that the city had "the worst paved streets I ever saw." In 1852 the editor of the *Louisville Daily Courier* advised that anyone traveling the plank road from Louisville to Portland "had better take a life preserver along," while in 1860 his counterpart at the *Louisville Daily Journal* suggested that the approaches to the city were "vile and execrable passwamps . . . in a most disgraceful condition." Major avenues in the center of town were in no better condition. "In one particular Louisville has gained an unenviable notoriety," the editor of the *Courier* charged. "We allude to the careless and dirty condition of the streets. In dry weather we are suffocated with constant clouds of dust, and in wet weather the streets are almost impassable on account of the accumulated mud and filth." Editor George D. Prentice of the *Journal* argued in a similar vein that Louisville's thoroughfares were either "uncommonly dusty" or so inundated that "skiffs would be useful conveyances to cross them." In July 1860 a draft authorizing the issuance of $1 million in bonds to be used for the improvement of streets and sewers was submitted to Louisville's General Council, which was once again preoccupied with "bouldering," paving, cleaning, and repairing the streets.

Municipal officials enacted ordinance after ordinance in a vain attempt to ease congestion and smooth the flow of traffic. As early as the 1780s Lexington's trustees ordered "all persons having cabins, cow pens, hog pens or other enclosures whatever within the main streets" of the city to remove them within sixty days. Louisville's trustees imposed fines for loitering, double parking, and galloping horses within the city limits. They forbade blacksmiths to shoe horses in the middle of the street, builders to block traffic with their equipment, and haulers to let wagons and vans stand for more than six hours while loading or unloading. But such legislation was routinely ignored, and streets remained choked with traffic and debris as congestion grew steadily worse. "One of the most thronged of our public thoroughfares is Market Street, between Third and Fourth," the editor of the *Louisville Daily Journal* announced in 1860. "There is a continual, in fact, unintermitting passage of vehicles. The paving contractors have deposited their heavy curbing stones and blockaded very nicely the entire street. It is barricaded equal to any of the Paris avenues during the revolutions of 1830, or that of 1848."

City streets were rarely cleaned, and their foul state evoked constant complaint from residents and travelers alike. In 1805 Louisville's trustees reported that the city's thoroughfares were cluttered with an assortment of "fire wood, . . . hog and pig fecus, dead animals, stable manure, [and] shavings and litter from buildings." During the same year the trustees of Lexington hired a free Negro named Davy to take four dead cows out of the street, while in 1811 officials in Louisville ordered watchmen to remove "all dead carcases . . . to some remote part of Town." Each of the many horses that passed through the towns relieved itself of between twenty and twenty-five pounds of manure a day. In wet weather the excrement turned streets into cesspools, while during dry spells it was refined into "pulverized horse dung" which blew "as a sharp, piercing powder" to cover people's clothes and irritate their eyes and nostrils. The trustees of Louisville enacted legislation to try to curb the numbers of "mad dogs" roaming the streets, and in 1828 the city officials offered a one-cent bounty for every rat killed and its scalp presented as evidence. (One citizen collected $1.36 for a single evening's work!) In his 1849 report to the American Medical Association on the "Sanitary Condition of Louisville," Dr. Lunsford Pitts Yandell declared that "it would certainly be difficult to find anywhere more uncleanly lanes and thoroughfares than Louisville exhibits. The refuse from the houses is deposited in the streets and alleys, and, with the filth produced by every other cause, is allowed to accumulate in heaps." By the eve of the Civil War conditions had not improved, and the editor of the *Louisville Daily Journal* argued that Market Street "is a perfect maelstrom and whirlpool of filth. All that alludes and effervesces from the lager beer saloons is deposited in the streets. There is garbage of every imaginable description of noxious substances. We are sure that our friend Dr. Weatherford, the Street Commissioner, if he ever passes that way, will elevate his nose to so great an angle that he will immediately set to work and have a cleansing of these Augean stables."

Residents of a typical frontier city wading through flooded
streets and battling swarms of rats, circa 1858

The early system by which individual householders and shop owners were responsible for sweeping the streets and removing nuisances broke down as rapid urbanization transformed hamlets into towns and cities. Local governments increasingly assumed responsibility for these services, hiring full-time street cleaners or appointing commissioners who organized their own crews. In 1813, for example, Lexington's trustees divided the city into ten wards or sanitary districts for "the purpose of employing scavengers to clean the streets of mud, dirt, filth &c." Ordinances were poorly enforced, however, and citizens became ever more aggravated. "We have had Hog Laws, Dog Laws, Theatre Laws, and Laws about the Hay Scale . . . Kitchen Slops, Soap Suds, and Filth of every kind, and in no single instance have they been executed," irate Lexingtonians charged.

In Kentucky cities, as in communities throughout the country, bands of hogs, protected by law and allowed to roam the streets to consume the garbage and refuse deposited in them, formed the first line of defense against filth. Charles Dickens visited Louisville and reported in 1842 that the streets were "perfectly alive with pigs of all ages, lying about in every direction fast asleep, or grunting along in quest of hidden dainties." Dickens was particularly interested in the peregrinations of "a very delicate porker with several straws sticking about his nose, betokening recent investigations in a dunghill." In 1850 Lady Emmeline Stuart-Wortley concluded that Louisville was evidently preparing for a "pronunciamento of pigs, they carry their snouts so high already, and seem so bristling with importance." Although residents occasionally complained when rampaging pigs ran down children in the street or crashed through parlor and storefront windows, town dwellers generally recognized the "Herculean" and indispensable service these animals performed and hence tolerated their presence.

During the early nineteenth century, progress in street cleaning was impeded by primitive methods of sanitation which were still largely those of the farm. Privies and water closets emptied into vaults and cesspools, and the waste products were either infrequently hauled away or allowed to soak into the soil to possibly contaminate water supplies. In Lexington, for example, the trustees feared in 1814 that the water table lay so close to the surface that cesspools threatened "to communicate with these wells . . . to jeopardize the health of our citizens." Fecal waste, urine, and kitchen slops were deposited in open drains which ran down either the middle or the sides of the streets and which depended upon rainfall and gravity to carry off the refuse. These primitive sewers were poorly constructed and became clogged with putrifying animal and vegetable matter when they were not dry. Angry residents constantly complained about the "filthiness of the gutters and sewers," the "greenish hue" of the accumulations, and the "noxious exhalations" which obstructed passage and endangered health. One Louisvillian recalled that on the eve of the Civil War pigs still roamed the downtown streets of the city and that "York Street . . . was an open sewer, possibly intended as a drain for that immediate locality."

At night, city streets were virtually pitch black. A few tavern owners and residents put their own oil lamps on the street in the early days, but since lamp-breaking became one of the more pop-

Pigs forage for food along Louisville's Market Street, 1856

ular outdoor sports among western teenagers, not many individuals took the risk. In 1819 McMurtrie observed that in Louisville "not a single lamp lends its cheering light to the nocturnal passenger, who frequently stands a good chance of breaking his neck." As late as 1860, "Reform," writing in the *Louisville Daily Courier,* complained that the condition of the streets was such "that it is hardly safe for a vehicle to pass in the night." While Lexington became the first frontier city to provide its citizens with a public lighting system in 1812, and Louisville became the first city in the West to provide gas lamps in 1837, most streets and thoroughfares remained without illumination. British visitor James Silk Buckingham reported in 1840 that in Louisville "the principal streets are lighted with gas; but by far the larger portion of the town is without lights or lamps."

Dark streets and alleys became increasingly unsafe as rising crime rates accompanied expanding population and wealth. Burgeoning commerce brought growing numbers of boisterous and semibarbarous transients to the cities—boatmen, adventurers, wagoners, drifters, migrant laborers, and ne'er-do-wells—described by contemporaries as "thoughtless, profligate, and degenerate" and "the most riotous and lawless set of people in America." When they hit town they spent much of their time gambling, carousing, fighting, drinking, consorting with "ladies of pleasure" and "nymphs of the pave," and terrorizing local inhabitants. This low life came to center in the grog shops, tippling houses, and brothels located on downtown streets and alleys, which formed small but ugly enclaves of vice and lawlessness. Havens for partially organized crime and the "dangerous classes," they harbored gangs of teenagers, criminals, and local riffraff who brutally assaulted local inhabitants and stole or destroyed their property. In 1820 a Louisville grand jury referred to a few downtown blocks as the "nurseries of vice and immorality" and the "sinks of society," and complained about "the great and unusual increase of tippling houses and houses of ill fame" in this district. Four years later a town meeting established a committee of thirty prominent citizens to "suppress" those engaged in "gambling, drunkenness, and other practices subversive to the peace, comfort and good order of society." No effective action followed, however, and complaints against this unsavory element continued to mount.

Lexington and Louisville early organized systems for police protection, supported largely or wholly by public funds, which became the most advanced in the West. The fear of Negroes and the desire to control growing urban slave populations seem to have been the primary incentives. In 1800, for example, Lexington expanded its watch to cover nights and Sundays when citizens complained that "large assemblages of Negroes [had] become troublesome to the Citizens," while Louisville added a fourth watchman to its patrol in 1826 with instructions "to be very particular as it regards collections of colored people . . . about the Market House and groceries." Louisville's trustees proclaimed that "it shall be the duty of the Watchmen as far as possible to prevent conflagrations, Felonies, Riots, routs, breaches of the peace and all unlawful assemblies of negroes." To carry out these tasks each watchman was armed with "a staff with a pike and hook on one end, a dark lantern, a rattle and trumpet, a small ladder and flambeau, a pair of scissors and a tin pot with a spout for the purpose of filling the lamps of this town with oil." So outfitted the night watchmen went about their rounds crying "in a shrill, unearthly tone, the time of night, and the weather." For undercover work Lexington hired "two confidential persons" and Louisville employed a "secret patrol."

Although these early police forces compared favorably with those in other cities, they were nevertheless small, untrained, poorly paid, ineffective against periodic waves of vandalism and major riots, and less than professional in their conduct. Poor enforcement was everywhere lamented, and Lexington authorities heard repeated allegations regarding the "improprieties," "delinquency," and "sundry misdemeanors and neglect of duty" of their watchmen. Local governments waged a constant battle to raise standards, maintain discipline, and improve morale, but with little success. Lexington officials in 1820 upbraided the captain of the watch for not breaking up a riot, fired the entire force five years later, and in 1827 received a petition attacking the chief "for sleeping in the watch house 6 to 8 hours in the night" and certain others who "sometimes intoxicate themselves with ardent spirits to the manifest injury of the public interest." In Louisville the trustees discharged almost every member of the patrol in 1822 and issued a call for "vigilant and temperate men." Seven years later they had to warn the guard not to "frequent the theatre, circus or any exhibition during watch hours," and had to fire one Peter Schwartz for the "improper treatment of an unprotected female." Teenagers and rowdies loved to "bait the watch," and even adults obstructed their work. In 1856, a year after Louisville's "Bloody Monday" nativist riot left between fourteen and one hundred persons dead and many more wounded and beaten, the city's General Council established a police department patterned after those in New York, Boston, and other eastern cities. The force consisted of a chief, his two assistants, eleven regular day watchmen, twenty-two regular night watchmen, and sixteen "supernumerary" watchmen. In spite of this change, the patrolmen continued to be largely undisciplined and incompetent, and the lives and property of the residents remained insecure.

Ineffective police forces also weakened the defenses of cities against fire, as the evening watch was designed in part to be an alarm system. Crowding increased as jerry-built structures were thrown together contiguously, and although the number of brick and stone houses rose steadily, builders continued to use wood extensively. The hastily constructed, closely packed buildings made fires difficult to contain, and primitive equipment worked badly or not at all. Arson early became a favorite weapon employed by disgruntled slaves. Small fires broke out so regularly that they received only passing notice in the newspapers, and serious conflagrations erupted with alarming frequency. In 1806 fire destroyed Hart and Dodge's rope factory in Lexington causing $8,000 in damages, and in 1827 flames swept through downtown Louisville destroying $20,000 worth of property. In the aftermath of the latter fire, the editor of the *Louisville Public Advertiser* admitted that "we are alike destitute of fire hooks and scaling ladders, and two of the three engines were out of repair." Looting must also have constituted a problem because "A Sufferer" wrote an open letter to the same newspaper stating that "he has no reason to believe, but that every individual who has become possessed of any of his property, will take the earliest occasion to return it." In 1840 the Falls City suffered a spectacular blaze that consumed thirty or more buildings worth approximately $300,000. The total damages from fire exceeded losses sustained in all other ways in these young cities, a fact reflected in the rates of the Kentucky Mutual Assurance Fire Company.

Initially the entire community was expected to respond to a fire, considered a city emergency, and residents were required to keep leather buckets in readiness. Lexington's trustees, for example, ordered all those between sixteen and sixty to appear at every blaze and form a bucket brigade. This system may have suited the needs of small villages, but it proved clumsy and impractical in rapidly growing cities, which turned increasingly to quasi-public volunteer fire companies. These volunteer companies were largely self-governing entities which were supported by city funds and equipment and by housing and other ordinances designed to minimize risks. The volunteer fire laddies, often dressed in colorful costumes, developed great *esprit de corps,* and their companies served more as social and political clubs than as the service organizations they were chartered to be. The various companies engaged in spirited and often bloody rivalries, and the "vamps" were frequently more interested in fighting each other than in battling the blaze. A Louisville observer remembered that "the dispositions on the part of one company to out-do another in valorous deeds and appear first upon the scene of a fire, often caused open hostilities while on their way to the conflagration, and the result was an abandonment of the apparatus and a general 'set to' until one or the other succumbed from mere exhaustion." In Louisville during 1855 a group belonging to a German hook and ladder company seriously injured a member of a rival company by pulling a ladder out from under him. Shortly thereafter, the members of the rival company set a trap for their antagonists by turning in a false alarm, then ambushed them, smashing their equipment and rolling it into the Ohio River. During the same year, after a newly built public school burned to the ground, the *Louisville Daily Journal* reported that the loss was due "more to lack of harmony among the several fire companies than want of water."

Local authorities increasingly assumed wider reponsibility for fire protection, screening applicants, supervising company finances, purchasing new pieces of equipment and keeping them in good repair, and generally circumscribing the independence of the volunteer companies. In 1858 Louisville's insurance underwriters forced the city's General Council to replace the unruly volunteer companies with a small, professional, paid fire department. The chief engineer of the new company boasted that this shift eliminated "the rioting and shedding of blood which have been attendant upon fire alarms, while the volunteer system was in existence."

Effective fire fighting depended in part on an ample supply of water, but rapidly growing cities frequently faced a crisis in provision of water both for battling blazes and for drinking. Kentucky cities early undertook to provide their citizens with water, erecting public wells equipped initially with a curb and buckets and later fitted with pumps. Pioneer settlers relied on these wells along with streams, springs, and rivers for their water supplies. Without the germ theory of disease to inform public opinion, early residents chose their drinking water on the basis of taste and appearance rather than purity. Although McMurtrie thought the Ohio an "extremely pure" river, he noted that Louisvillians preferred well water, which he found "extremely bad, containing, besides a considerable quantity of lime, a large portion of decomposed vegetable matter." The construction of a water works in the Falls City would not begin until 1857, and the system would not be placed in operation until 1860.

Pools of stagnant water posed an additional problem for Louisville, Henderson, and other Kentucky communities. Louisville in particular suffered from these "depots of universal mischief," which brought sickness during the summer months and gave the city its reputation as the "graveyard" of the Ohio Valley. Richard Clough Anderson, Jr., wrote in his diary in 1815 that the "fatal sickliness of the place . . . must continue until the ponds are drained of stagnant water." In 1822 several hundred Louisvillians perished in a tragic yellow fever epidemic which, in the words of Dr. Daniel Drake, "scoured [the city] almost to desolation." The editor of the *Louisville Public Advertiser* again complained about the ponds, "those intolerable and life destroying nuisances," while the following year Italian visitor J.C. Beltrami observed that "a great number of the inhabitants [of this town] yearly fall a sacrifice to the pestilential exhalations of the surrounding marshes." For the next six years the effort to drain the ponds became the chief business of the town, and other projects were cut back or postponed. The state authorized a $60,000 lottery in 1823 to help finance the project, the Louisville Theatre held benefit performances for the "Pond Fund," and a town engineer was appointed to superintend the draining effort. By 1849, Dr. Lunsford Pitts Yandell could assert that "within the city limits [the ponds] are nowhere to be seen," but he admitted that "south of the city, and extending twenty miles . . . , is a district of country known by the ominous name of the 'Pond Settlement.'"

Fetid pools of stagnant water, poor sanitation, shortages of pure water, overcrowding, erroneous beliefs about the causes of disease, and a laissez-faire governmental tradition which made measures of public control difficult, all contributed to the most terrifying problem in the early history of Kentucky cities—

epidemic. Although endemic diseases such as malaria and tuberculosis regularly killed far more inhabitants than did the periodic waves of pestilence, it was the spectacular presence of plague that produced a widespread awareness of the filthy and unhealthful conditions in the cities and contributed to concerted efforts to bring about sanitary reform. Communities at first reacted to epidemics by hastily setting up haphazard and temporary boards of health that disappeared with the diseases that had brought them into being. In 1822, for example, Louisville established a board of health and invested it with the responsibility to secure the city "from the evils, distresses, and calamities of contagious, malignant, and infectious diseases." But as early as May 1823 the editor of the *Louisville Public Advertiser,* concerned about the possibility of another outbreak of yellow fever, charged that "no sooner are we completely over the effects of a 'spell of sickness,' than avarice seems to resume her sway, and each man begins to look out for himself." Five decades later municipalities recognized their obligation to maintain permanent boards of health invested with sweeping powers to curtail the liberties of individuals in order to protect the welfare of the community. Fear of epidemic disease, and the growing realization that epidemics could be prevented through sanitary measures, more than any other factors worked to modify the extreme individualism that early city dwellers had brought with them from rural and frontier areas.

Asiatic cholera was the classic epidemic disease of the nineteenth century, as bubonic plague had been of the fourteenth. It struck the United States in 1832, 1849, 1866, and 1873, the period during which public health and sanitary engineering were straining to catch up with rapid urbanization and the transportation revolution. Cholera was spread through contaminated water supplies, but neither the cause nor the etiology of the disease were known at the time. (It was not until 1883 that Robert Koch isolated the *Vibrio cholerae,* the motile, comma-shaped bacillus that caused cholera.) The highly explosive character of the epidemic outbreaks and the spectacular symptoms of the disease spread fear and panic in Kentucky, as elsewhere. Cholera had a short incubation period and a high fatality rate, and its symptoms were strikingly similar to those of acute arsenical poisoning. Diarrhea, acute spasmodic vomiting, and severe abdominal cramps led rapidly to dehydration, cyanosis, and frequently death. Individuals who appeared quite well in the morning could be dead by nightfall, and physicians were largely helpless in the face of a plague they could neither understand nor cure.

When Asiatic cholera first struck Kentucky in the years between 1832 and 1835, it spread terror and confusion along with illness and death. Thousands fled cities and towns in a "perfect stampede," but cholera infected rural areas as well, leaving one frightened Lexingtonian to relate that "when I thought of flight, I knew not where to go—the country [was] filled with cholera." As the demand for coffins outstripped the supply, the bodies of cholera victims were hastily deposited in jumbled heaps at cemetery gates in boxes, trunks, and even the bed linens in which they had died. The dead were frequently buried in long, shallow trenches, producing an unmistakable and unforgettable stench. "Great fear fell over the people [of Danville] and paleness spread over every face," Dr. J.J. Polk recalled. A Lexington newspaper editor confessed that "the stoutest hearts seemed to quail before the relentless destroyer . . . [and everyone] seemed to be seized with an awful dread." During the summer of 1833, one-third of Lexington's population fled and over 500 residents of the city died. An unidentified Lexingtonian observed that "the distress is beyond description! No city police,—(at least not visible)—no board of health—no medical reports—and the streets have for the most part the stillness which pervades the ruins of Palmyra. . . . The markets are suspended and the bakers' shops shut, with one exception. Not a pound of beef to be got—and very little else. Not even a cracker for sale. . . . I leave you to imagine the picture of our despair." A Russellville woman wrote two years later that "every description of business made a full stop. The printer and all the magistrates died, the postmaster and clerks were at the point of death, every store shut up, their owners either dead or fled into the country. I have never seen such a scene of calamity in my life."

Most physicians subscribed to the miasmatic theory of disease, believing that illness was spread by poisonous gases or "pestilential exhalations" emanating from rotting organic and vegetable matter, decaying garbage and filth, and fetid pools of stagnant water. Although this environmentalist theory of disease was unsound, it nevertheless provided a strong argument for cleaning up cities and for instituting sanitary and health reforms. In June 1832 the editor of the *Louisville Public Advertiser* urged local authorities to emulate the preventative efforts of Philadelphia and Cincinnati by inaugurating a campaign to "clean and purify the city" and "cleanse our streets and alleys from every impurity." He warned that "no expense, no pains should be spared to accomplish this object. The lives of our citizens should not be sacrificed to a cold calculation of dollars and cents. Precautionary steps cannot be taken too soon—when pestilence shall be seen stalking through our city, and filling our dwellings with desolation and death, it will be too late to begin the work . . . recommended by every consideration of humanity." Despite such warnings, the initial cholera outbreak in Kentucky did not excite city or state officials to enact sanitary measures to prevent the return of the pestilence.

When news of cholera's return to the United States in 1849 reached Kentucky, however, a few communities embarked on organized clean-up campaigns as preventative measures. Covington's municipal officials, at the urging of the community's physicians, divided the city into districts and established a board of health for each area. These boards were to supervise the cleaning of cellars, privies, stables, backyards, streets, gutters, and sewers, to provide for drainage of nearby ponds, to use whitewash, lime, and nitrate of lead to disinfect and remove offensive odors from cleansed areas, to establish dispensaries where the poor could obtain free medical advice, and to keep accurate morbidity and mortality statistics. The clean-up campaign was credited with preventing a serious epidemic in Covington. In Louisville, when cholera broke out in the same filthy section of riverfront dwellings and warehouses that had been most severely stricken in 1832, the mayor and city council appointed a board of health and charged it to improve conditions throughout the city but especially to scour that foul area. Several Louisvillians who refused to clean their yards were placed under arrest. The clean-up campaign continued through the fall and winter, and when cholera returned during the summer of 1850, no cases were reported in the newly cleansed area. On June 16, 1850, the editor of the *Louisville Journal* referred to Asiatic cholera as "a health inspector that speaks in a language that no one can misunderstand."

Although in 1832 some Kentuckians viewed cholera as "a dispensation of Divine Justice in consequence of our national and individual sins," as the Kentucky Conference of Methodist Preachers proclaimed, the scourge increasingly came to be seen by inhabitants of the cities as a byproduct of remediable faults in sanitation. Between 1849 and 1854 London physician John Snow proved experimentally that cholera was spread through contaminated water and that, even though it still could not be cured, it *could* be *prevented* through disinfection and quarantine. In 1866 New York City established its Metropolitan Board of Health, and the agency's achievements reinforced the growing conviction that cities had an obligation to vigorously enforce sanitary regulations to protect the public health, circumscribing designated individual freedoms where necessary. "When 125,000 people are gathered together on 10 square miles of land they must of necessity give up certain of their liberties," Dr. Charles V. Chapin, a pioneering champion of public health, contended. "It is the sacrifice they make for the advantages of city life." As historian Charles E. Rosenberg pointed out, cholera acted as a catalyst in helping "to bring about the creation of the public health reforms demanded by the almost unendurable conditions of the nineteenth-century city." By fits and starts, Kentucky cities moved to embrace the gospel of public health, establish permanent and powerful boards of health, and enforce standards of cleanliness and healthfulness.

In 1873 Asiatic cholera returned for its final visit to the United States. Although the pestilence probably ravaged Kentucky more severely than any other state in the union, most of the larger cities across the state remained relatively unscathed, and Lexington reported no cases of the disease at all. But residents of small towns and villages had not learned the lessons that cholera had so profoundly impressed upon urban inhabitants, and they suffered accordingly. Columbia, Kentucky, a hamlet of 600, was devastated by the pestilence in 1873, and some charged that the truculence of a few individuals "proved to be the cause of much suffering." The owner of a particularly vile hotel and stable stubbornly insisted that the request of authorities that he clean up his establishment represented an "unwarranted interference with his property." Two months after cholera had spread through his hotel and local authorities had ordered it closed and disinfected, a visitor inspecting the hotel rooms in which victims of the pestilence had died discovered that the quarters had been neither cleaned nor disinfected. The error of not having cleansed these rooms was "most earnestly impressed upon the person in charge of the property, with the only result of eliciting an expression of displeasure at such interference—a closing demonstration of the same foolish obstinacy that had subjected the town to a fearful epidemic" that had killed one hundred of Columbia's inhabitants.

As the cholera years drew to a close, the cities in the Commonwealth were increasingly replacing casual, semiprivate systems for provision of basic urban services with formal, publicly financed and governmentally operated programs. The magnitude and urgency of the first urban crisis had bred civic responsibility, leadership, and a new kind of urban statesmanship. Municipalities had begun to experiment on a modest scale with long-range programs and city-wide planning, reflecting a growing awareness of the interdependence and scope of the problems. Asiatic cholera had come as "a health inspector that speaks in a language that no one can misunderstand." It had taught that municipal government had the obligation to expand its powers in order to provide essential services and protect the general welfare. And it had taught that, in the words of one city health officer, "good privies are far higher signs of civilization than grand palaces and fine art galleries."

4

VISIONS OF METROPOLIS

AT THE CLOSE of the Civil War, both Louisville and Cincinnati impatiently stood ready to reopen trade with the South and to renew their economic rivalry with each other. On April 29, 1865, the editor of the *Louisville Daily Journal* announced that "we deem it a matter of the utmost importance that the freedom of trade [with the South] should be established at the earliest day possible which may be consistent with the idea of withholding supplies from the enemy." He warned Falls City merchants that "none of our natural tributaries must be diverted from us by superior inducements, either in price or transportation, which may be offered by our competitors." Several weeks later he cautioned that "we may rest assured that other communities will not remain idle. Chicago, Cincinnati, St. Louis, etc., will be astir, and unless we intend to surrender at discretion and give up this new contest without an effort, we had better gird up our loins for the friendly fight without a moment's delay." In fact, the Cincinnati Chamber of Commerce had already passed a resolution calling upon the federal government to restore commerce in noncontraband articles with the South as expeditiously as possible. In both cities developers with grandiose visions of metropolis were eager to get on with the business of town building and urban promotion.

Louisville's commercial success, after the Civil War as before it, stemmed in large measure from the willingness of the city's leading merchants and men of affairs to devote their time, money, and energy to enterprises designed to stimulate growth. Like businessmen elsewhere, they displayed tenacious urban loyalties and a fierce brand of civic patriotism, believing that personal ambition and community welfare were intimately related. As historian Daniel J. Boorstin observed, the American businessman's "starting belief was in the interfusing of public and private prosperity. . . . Not to boost your city showed both a lack of community spirit and a lack of business sense. . . . Here was a new breed: the community builder in a mushrooming city where personal and public growth, personal and public prosperity intermingled." In this spirit the Falls City's business leaders contributed financial support to railroads, packet lines, and river transportation improvement projects. They mapped out defensive strategies to thwart the schemes of economic rivals, formulated promotional campaigns, sponsored community projects, directed mercantile organizations, and influenced corporation directorates. They also filled most of the important positions in local politics from their own ranks, thereby insuring that Louisville's municipal government would be responsive to their needs. After the war these merchants and entrepreneurs had to adjust to three important changes in the nature of the southern trade: the partial collapse of the plantation economy, the rise of the southern country store, and the continuing decline of long-haul river commerce. As historian Leonard P. Curry demonstrated, the Louisville business community's creative response to these challenges sparked an impressive surge in trade and enabled the Falls City to sustain its drive for commercial empire in the South.

Louisville merchants recognized earlier than most that the commercial importance of the Ohio and Mississippi rivers would continue to decline and that the age of the palatial steamboat had passed. They perceived the beginnings of a new era in river navigation in which fast packet boats would play a major role, making frequent trips on tributary waterways and serving as feeders to the railroads. In 1867 Louisville's Board of Trade signed contracts to support the establishment of scheduled packet lines on the Arkansas, Tennessee, and White rivers. A subsidy of more than $20,000 was raised by subscription, and board members promised to give preference to these boats in shipping their merchandise. In June

1868 the editor of the *Louisville Daily Journal* gloated that the lines on the Arkansas and the White had already "succeeded in breaking up the business intercourse . . . that existed between Arkansas merchants and St. Louis, Memphis, and New Orleans merchants. . . . Most generously have [the merchants and farmers of the area] manifested their appreciation by giving in return a larger portion of their trade to Louisville than to any other city."

The altered circumstances of the southern trade also prompted Louisville merchants to develop innovative marketing methods. Their most important customers were no longer the plantation owners who had formerly come to them, but rather country storekeepers who needed to be visited regularly at their own establishments. Louisville wholesale houses responded to this change by dispatching commercial agents known as drummers to every town and crossroads village between the Falls of the Ohio and Montgomery, Alabama. These traveling salesmen were imbued with the prevailing civic patriotism and worked as hard to further the commercial interests of the city as to augment their own commissions. One contemporary acknowledged that throughout the southern states it was well known that "if a [Louisville] hardware drummer could sell a consignment of groceries for a Louisville house, he always took the order and passed it on to the Louisville groceryman." Historian James P. Sullivan concluded that "the Board of Trade looked upon the drummers as missionaries who in carrying the gospel of trade represented 'Main Street' as well as their individual houses."

Many of Louisville's drummers were ex-Confederates, for the community's merchants recognized that the city's "southernness" could be an important psychological weapon in the battle with Cincinnati for the trade of the South. Louisvillians frequently characterized their city as a "live western town" as distinguished from an "old fogy city in the East" when discussing its civic virtues in either a local or a national context. But they invariably depicted their community as a southern metropolis when directing appeals to potential customers in Dixie. Falls City publicists and promoters courted southern business by emphasizing Louisville's location within a former slave state, proclaiming the city's identity of interest with the South, and vilifying Cincinnati for its alleged

"Yankee" proclivities. As early as January 1866 the *Louisville Industrial and Commercial Gazette* declared that southern merchants should trade with Louisville "because money spent at home—in the South—is money saved, while money spent abroad is gone forever," and "because in Louisville they can deal with their life-long friends and neighbors, who are here doing business from every part of the South." While this appeal for the trade of the South also contained arguments based on competitive prices and superior transportation facilities, a similar entreaty published eighteen months later in the *Louisville Daily Journal* emphasized the city's southern ties almost exclusively. "Since the close of the war, our merchants have acted toward those of the South in a spirit of truest magnanimity," the editor proclaimed. "This generous example has scarcely had one imitator in the opulent cities of Cincinnati, Philadelphia, New York, or Boston, whose merchants have enjoyed and grown fat on the custom of the South in years past. . . . [Louisville] is the metropolis of a gallant Southern State claiming full identity of blood and interest with the whole sunny cordon."

As Radical Reconstruction deepened southern distrust of all things northern, Louisville propagandists intensified their appeals to defensive regional loyalties. Cincinnati was branded a "hotbed of radicalism" and a "northern city that has aided to rob us of half of our property." In September 1870, several weeks before a "Southern Commercial Convention" was due to convene in Cincinnati, *Courier-Journal* editor Henry Watterson protested that "to locate a Southern Convention there is doing violence to all outline maps of geography, common sense, history, and decency. There is nothing Southern in or about Cincinnati. In all the broad Southern land it is on record that Cincinnati is Southern, precisely as the carpet-baggers are Southern. She now reaches out her long, bony fingers for . . . Southern dollars and cents, just as she reached them out during the war for Southern cotton and Southern plantations." When Robert E. Lee died less than a month later and obituaries in Cincinnati newspapers labeled the Confederate general a "traitor," Watterson thundered that "the people of the South will remember Cincinnati. They ought to remember it. Among the cities of the North it has signalized itself the most vindictive, and this with the less excuse, because its malice is gratuitous and brutal, displaying itself at the wine table and at the open grave; and treacherous likewise, because but a fortnight ago the men who are now bawling 'rebel' and 'traitor' had their hands in our pockets and were whining 'friends' and 'brothers,' whilst they picked them." Louisvillians lost no opportunity to use propaganda as a tactical weapon to strengthen their city's ties to the South and to weaken those of the Queen City, and there were indications that the desired results were being achieved. Journalist Charles Dudley Warner reported that "sentiment does play a considerable part in business, and it is within the knowledge of the writer that prominent merchants . . . have refused trade contracts, that should have been advantageous to Cincinnati, on account of this partisan spirit, as if the war were not over."

Louisville entrepreneurs recognized that, while propaganda could give their city an advantage in its trade rivalries with Cincinnati and other communities, in the long run success would depend upon the continued and vigorous prosecution of an ambitious transportation program. The city's business leaders early concluded that railroads would be the decisive weapons in the struggle for southern commerce in the post-Civil War era. In April 1867 the editor of the *Louisville Daily Journal* declared that "we must rely upon railroads, more than ever, to develop and restore the country. . . . The iron horse is king. Railroads are the great civilizers and developers of cities, states, and nations." The city's businessmen encouraged the L&N to consolidate and extend its network south and southeast of Nashville, to establish fast freight connections between the Falls City and the South, and to construct new rail lines to tap markets in central and western Kentucky. The city continued its pre-Civil War policy of purchasing corporation stock with community funds, subscribing $1 million to the L&N in 1867 and $1 million to the Elizabethtown and Paducah Railroad in 1868. By the end of 1868 Louisville had issued more than $3.5 million in bonds to aid various railroad projects radiating out into the city's commercial hinterland.

The city of Louisville supported railroads in part as defensive weapons to undermine the transportation plans of economic rivals. For example, Falls City entrepreneurs sponsored the Elizabethtown and Paducah Railroad in order to frustrate the bid of Evansville, Indiana, to siphon off some of the southern trade by constructing a railroad south through Henderson, Kentucky, and connecting with the Memphis branch of the L&N. "Already Evansville, a small but thriving city in a foreign state, is preparing to grasp the prize that should by all fair means belong to Louisville," the editor of the *Louisville Daily Journal* warned in April 1867. "The road now projected from Evansville to Nashville, tapping the Edgefield and Kentucky road at its intersection with the Memphis and Clarksville road, . . . will cut short all intercourse between us and our imploring friends in Hardin, Grayson, Muhlenberg, Caldwell, and other intervening and adjoining counties. The only effectual check that can be put upon the Evansville scheme is to build the road from Elizabethtown to Paducah." The railroad would have the additional advantage of expanding Louisville's market in western Kentucky, where as one traveler had reported there were "a great many Kentucky merchants buying their goods in Evansville, that should be induced to make their purchases in Louisville."

Louisville's city council also authorized a subscription of $100,000 in March 1867 to a branch line of the Louisville and Nashville to run from Stanford to Richmond, in order to stymie the plans of Cincinnati interests to build a line from Lexington through Richmond to a point on the Lebanon branch of the L&N near Mount Vernon. "Our belief," the editor of the *Louisville Daily Journal* announced, "is that if [the people of Madison, Garrard, and Lincoln counties] do not guard well their assailable points, they will be worse victimized by wily Cincinnati than even Boyle county has been. We caution them to repudiate the lovemaking of Cincinnati. . . . The true interests of these counties lie in the direction of Louisville." Even though the people of Madison County "had been divided by the machinations of vulture-like Cincinnati and her aiders and abettors in Lexington," ultimately "victory was seen to perch upon the standard of Progress, and defeat was emblazoned upon the trailing banners of Old-fogyism." The editor of the *Cincinnati Times* complained that "there seems to have come upon the stage of Kentucky life a race of dwarfs that take a very minute view of public affairs, and exhibit a puerile incapacity to comprehend great results that are embosomed in the immediate future."

Cincinnati railroad interests had "aiders and abettors in Lexington" in part because Louisville's efforts to deny the Queen City rail access to southern markets had the effect of denying the Bluegrass region rail lines as well. Despite the postwar spurt in railroad construction, by the early 1870s Kentucky still had fewer miles of track in proportion to its size than most neighboring states, and to the south and east of Lexington rail lines were practically nonexistent. Although this deficiency could have been blamed as much on shortages of capital as on the defensive tactics of Louisville's mercantile community, residents of the Bluegrass region looked upon the Falls City as the primary source of their transportation miseries. Irate central Kentuckians threatened to cut off trade with the "dull, stale, flat and miasmatic city of Louisville," and zealously supported the Cincinnati Southern Railroad bill in the Kentucky legislature. "Now we do most fervently wish that foreigners would come in and build us roads everywhere through the state and run them for us," the editor of Lexington's *Kentucky Gazette* wailed in February 1870. "If Cincinnati will build us a railroad, then, in the name of God, let her have a charter properly guarded and let her have such aid from the counties as they may think the road is worth to them." Forecasting victory, he predicted that Louisville "will have reaped a harvest of odium which will stick to her like the leprosy of Gehazi, and the people of the South will avoid her marts as if a pestilence were raging in her streets."

Throughout this era, small towns in Kentucky attempted to exploit the rivalry between Louisville and Cincinnati in order to acquire the precious rail connections which might enable them to realize their own visions of metropolis. In the summer of 1866, for example, residents of Somerset and Stanford tried to spur the further extension of the Lebanon branch of the L&N past Crab Orchard. A resident of Somerset suggested that "the energetic manner in which this road has been pushed forward to Crab Orchard, and the promise it gives of continuing to the Tennessee line, should disturb, if it does not wake, from their lethargic sleep the old fogy, Rip Van Winkle merchants of the Queen City. . . . Will

Kentucky enterprise continue this road to the mountains and catch from Cincinnati's grasp the commerce of that section?" Danville promoters eager to entice the L&N to build a branch line to their community argued that "it is for the interest of Louisville that the road be put through at once, in order to secure the trade before Cincinnati can reach that important point." The officials of the Tuscumbia and Opelika Railroad assured the Falls City's Board of Trade that the completion of their line "would *impregnably* fortify Louisville against the possibility of successful trade rivalry on the part of Cincinnati, for the trade of South Alabama and Georgia." Similarly, the proponents of a railroad from Louisville to Norfolk, Virginia, via the Cumberland Gap, declared that "it would soon make Louisville the peer of Cincinnati in all respects, and give her superiority in some." Others claimed that Louisville would surely surpass Cincinnati if Falls City entrepreneurs would only recognize the wisdom of helping to construct a railroad from Elizabethtown to Greensburg, or from Gallatin, Tennessee, to Lebanon, Tennessee, or from Elizabethtown to McMinnville, Tennessee.

Owensboro's "dream of glory" during these years centered upon building a railroad to Russellville. "We must get up more steam, and send the 'iron horse' over the plains and through the hills of this rich but underdeveloped country," the editor of the *Owensboro Monitor* announced in 1866. "A road from here to Russellville is of the utmost importance to this whole section of the country." One Owensboroan asserted that the line was necessary to insure that the community would become "the first city in point of population and wealth between Louisville and Memphis," and he warned his fellow citizens not to "let Evansville and Henderson entirely eclipse us." In 1867, when the General Assembly chartered the Owensboro and Russellville Railroad and voters approved the Daviess County Court's purchase of $250,000 worth of stock in the line, the *Monitor*'s editor was overjoyed. "THE PEOPLE SPEAK," he exulted, "and the Shriek of the Iron Horse Responds!" Chronic financial problems, however, caused delays, bankruptcies, and reorganizations. The road was ultimately completed to Russellville, enabling Owensboro to tap the rich coal, timber, and agricultural areas of Daviess, McLean, Muhlenberg, and Logan counties, but the lofty dreams of the city's prophets of destiny were not realized.

In April 1879 *Courier-Journal* editor Henry Watterson perceived his own city's metropolitan dreams in jeopardy. In an impassioned address to Louisville's leading merchants and manufacturers, he exhorted the businessmen to launch a counterattack against the community's adversaries before it was too late. "Time was," he declared, "when holding the one great railway artery that extended itself into the South, we could afford to look with complacence upon the fruitless wriggling and dolorous writhing of our rivals. That time is gone. Cincinnati to the right of us, St. Louis to the left of us, Chicago in front of us—sending their volleys into flank, face and rear—it behooves us to shake ourselves. . . . I see danger on every hand. Injuns on the upper road and Death upon the lower. The time has come to realize the situation . . . so that every man may be around to put his shoulder to the wheel."

Watterson might well have added 'Nashville to the south of us.' For between 1879 and 1880 Louisville faced a new challenge from the Tennessee capital in the form of a grandiose scheme involving the Nashville, Chattanooga and St. Louis Railroad and a contemplated trunk line from St. Louis to Savannah. The directors of the Nashville railroad, much of which would parallel the L&N, denounced the Louisville railway as a "foreign corporation" whose "aggressive policy" made it "a menace to the rights of this company." Edmund W. "King" Cole, the dynamic president of the Nashville line, purchased controlling interest in the unfinished and moribund Owensboro and Nashville Railroad in July 1879 and proceeded with his plans to acquire other rail connections through Georgia. Suddenly, however, in January 1880 the L&N acquired enough stock in the Nashville, Chattanooga and St. Louis to gain control of the line. In one brilliant maneuver the L&N both eliminated a dangerous rival and absorbed "King" Cole's entire system. The *Courier-Journal* rejoiced that "the scoop of the Nashville, Chattanooga and St. Louis is a stroke of magnificent railroad diplomacy," termed the take-over "a *coup de chemin de fer*," and sneered that "King Cole was a monarch dethroned as Nashville weeped." The newspaper compared

President Elisha D. Standiford and Vice-President H. Victor Newcomb of the L&N to "Kaiser Wilhelm and Count [Otto] von Bismarck," respectively, and proclaimed that the two railroad men were "making a 'United Germany' of the Southern railways which were lying about loose . . . instead of leading to Louisville as they should." The *Nashville Banner* complained about "the supreme and unparalleled impertinence of Louisville," charging that the Kentucky emporium had been a "two faced Janus" whose most consistent policy was its "frog like puff and strut." The *Banner* branded Louisville a "shoddy, codfish city" which with its "usual low cunning" had turned both itself and its railroad over to the Yankees during the Civil War. When Louisvillians boasted that their achievement represented a major victory over Cincinnati as well, the *Banner* ridiculed the notion. "The notion of little Louisville comparing herself to Cincinnati and talking of making Cincinnati tributary to her reminds one of what the rooster said in the stable with the horses, 'Be careful, gentlemen, don't let us step on each other.' "

Following the take-over of the Nashville, Chattanooga and St. Louis Railroad, Louisville's Board of Trade passed a resolution congratulating the management of the L&N for having pursued "so masterly a policy, consolidating as it does a truly imperial system of roads, and enhancing the importance of Louisville as a railroad center." In the years following the conclusion of the Civil War, the L&N had acquired control of no less than nineteen railroads and had become a regional giant stretching from the Falls of the Ohio to the Gulf of Mexico. By the summer of 1880 the Louisville and Nashville system controlled directly or indirectly some 2,348 miles of track, and railroad circles buzzed with news of the breathtaking expansion of the railway. "Only a short time ago the Louisville and Nashville could have been described with tolerable accuracy as simply a line extending from Louisville to Memphis in one direction, and from Louisville through Nashville to Montgomery, Alabama, in another direction," one observer reported in the *Commercial and Financial Chronicle* in April 1880. "It now . . . extends from St. Louis, Louisville, Evansville, Hickman, and Memphis, to New Orleans, Mobile, Pensacola, and Savannah, and touches such important points as Nashville, Chattanooga,

Selma, Montgomery, Eufaula, Columbus, Macon, Atlanta, and Augusta. . . . It is not to be wondered at that a combination so vast as this should excite jealousy, and give rise to schemes for the formation of opposition lines."

After 1880 there were significant changes in the organization of the L&N, in the political leadership of the Falls City, and in the structure of Louisville's economy. Until that date, the Board of Directors of the railroad had been made up largely of local businessmen. But at the 1880 stockholders meeting "outsiders" representing New York and British investors were elected to the board, and five years later the city of Louisville sold its stock in the corporation. The city's close economic ties to the South had been weakened by a number of developments. The completion of the Cincinnati Southern Railroad to Chattanooga in February 1880 had destroyed the L&N's twenty-year monopoly over through traffic between the Ohio River and the Gulf of Mexico. The L&N, with extensions to the northeast and to the northwest, had ceased to be an exclusively southern railway. The South itself had become more self-reliant, drawing on its own resources and on other cities both within and outside the region's borders. And Louisville merchants and manufacturers had begun to develop outlets for their wares beyond the South. After 1880 industry became relatively more important in the city's economy, and commercial interests lost the political power they had exercised for so many decades. Professional politicians began to assume positions in municipal government, while businessmen with ties to manufacturing and production took over the leadership of the Board of Trade. As railroads had earlier superseded steamboats, so industry had begun to overshadow commerce in the economic life of the Falls City.

Throughout the late nineteenth and early twentieth centuries, Louisville experienced an impressive expansion of its industrial sector. In 1875 a local writer proclaimed that "the secret of substantial and steady growth is found in workshops teeming with mechanics and laborers." By 1885 an estimated 22,000 operatives worked in some 1,300 manufacturing establishments and annually produced goods valued at $50 million. Pork packing, tobacco manufacturing, and whiskey distilling remained the city's leading industries, prompting Henry Watterson to boast that "a union of pork, tobacco and whiskey will make us all wealthy, healthy and frisky." Industrialists organized new and varied manufacturing concerns, erected large-scale factories, and replaced small, family-owned firms with giant corporations. In 1883 the people of Louisville set out to "secure the greatest Industrial Exposition ever held in America," and launched the Southern Exposition, which ran for five years. Watterson hailed "the beginning of a new industrial era" in the city's history, and the central feature of the succeeding decades was the growth and development of Louisville's manufacturing sector. In 1927 a report in *Forbes* magazine concluded that "Louisville, when she started her boosting, employed the slogan 'Gateway to the South.' She still employs it, but more and more she is now using 'Premier Industrial Location' instead. For Louisville, still sentimentally attached to the South, has discovered that modern industry . . . is not a matter of geography. . . . A gateway, moreover, can not be open in the one direction without being open in the other. Louisville is finding herself equally a gateway to the North, and her prosperity is all tied up with prosperity in every other section."

As a thriving regional metropolis and a gateway to both North and South, Louisville needed an impressive city gate. This need was fulfilled by the Louisville and Nashville Railroad's Union Station, a magnificent cathedral-like structure completed in 1891 and the first monumental and architecturally significant railway station in the South. The Romanesque exterior of light gray, heavy-cut rusticated stone featured a soaring clock tower, spires and turrets, and two leaded, stained-glass rose windows. The waiting room displayed a mosaic tile floor, polished brass and marble fixtures, carved Corinthian capitals on the interior columns, and a stained-glass skylight. One editor explained that "when it is remembered that a railway station is the entrance door to a town, . . . and all who enter the town get their first impression there, we begin to see how important the terminal is."

During the great age of city growth between 1880 and 1930, railway stations built as Romanesque cathedrals, Gothic castles, and Roman baths served as the architectural embodiments of corporate prosperity and the physical symbols of urban maturity. This was the "age of the great depots," when, as historian Keith L. Bryant, Jr., observed, "steel, iron, brick, and glass merged in monumental structures to provide visual proof of metropolitan

The L&N's Union Station, Louisville, completed in 1891

progress." The railway station was the ideal symbol of urban development, for the iron horse enabled cities to expand their hinterlands and to tap new markets, carried the commercial and industrial products of an urban age to distant localities, and tied together an emerging national network of cities and towns. "Railway termini and hotels are to the nineteenth century what monasteries and cathedrals were to the thirteenth century," the editor of the *Building News* of London declared in 1875. "They are truly the only real representative kind of building we possess."

The "age of the great depots" was also the great era of "the rise of the city"—the period during which burgeoning metropolises erected not only magnificent railway stations but huge public buildings, giant factories, and gleaming skyscrapers. Americans generally celebrated urbanization as the hallmark of material growth and progress, and hailed great cities as the preeminent symbols of a rising standard of living and of the emergence of the United States as a powerful industrial nation. These were the decades during which the lure of the city became compelling to hundreds of thousands of restless rural youngsters, who moved to the cities seeking adventure, romance, and success. Novelist Harold Frederic, himself swept up in this massive cityward tide, caught the essence of the age in 1887. "The nineteenth century is a century of cities," Frederic wrote; "they have given their own twist to the progress of the age—and the farmer is as far out of it as if he lived in Alaska. Perhaps there was a time when a man could live in what the poet calls daily communication with nature and not starve his mind and dwarf his soul, but this isn't the century."

Between 1870 and 1930 thousands of Kentuckians joined the nationwide migration to the cities. By the latter year 800,000 Kentuckians, representing almost one-third of the state's entire population, lived in the fifty-three urban places of 2,500 people or more, and thirteen cities in the Commonwealth registered populations in excess of 10,000 inhabitants. A number of new cities developed as satellites of such established centers as Louisville in Jefferson County and Covington and Newport in northern Kentucky. Throughout the period the intensification of urbanization led to the rise of cities in portions of the state previously untouched by the process. During the late nineteenth century, Princeton, Providence, and Morganfield began to develop in west-central Kentucky, and Mayfield, Fulton, and Murray sprang up in the far western section of the Commonwealth. In the southeastern corner of the state, Middlesboro, Somerset, Pineville, Corbin, and Williamsburg were planted before 1900, while during the opening decades of the new century the eastern and southeastern sections witnessed the beginnings of Jenkins, Hazard, Harlan, Lynch, Barbourville, Wayland, Elkhorn City, Pikeville, Prestonsburg, Van Lear, and Paintsville. Between 1900 and 1930 Dawson Springs, Greenville, and Sturgis began to grow in west-central

Kentucky. Some of the mountain towns were overgrown mining camps dominated by a single great mining company, as Jenkins, Lynch, Benham, and Stearns. Other mountain communities, although primarily dependent upon coal mining, developed independently of a single mining company and built up manufacturing establishments such as lumber mills, canning factories, and clay working plants which relied heavily upon local resources.

One town developed by a single corporation was Lynch, located in the heart of a magnificent coal field in Harlan County. In 1917 the United States Coal and Coke Company, a subsidiary of the United States Steel Corporation, set up a mining camp, opened a coal mine, extended railroad tracks toward the locality, and began to build a town. "At the far northern end of the county the greatest corporation in the world was creating a city overnight," a contemporary remarked in 1920, "blasting its streets into the side of the mountains, moving a river from side to side of the valley, erecting a metropolitan hotel where stood a log cabin barely two years ago, bending every resource of large capital and the trained intelligence which money can buy to the making of a modern town." Between 1917 and 1925 a complete town was constructed that covered all of the available valley and climbed both sides of the mountain. Lynch had churches, schools, a hospital, an amusement center, a hotel, a company store, 600 houses, ten miles of paved streets, and over twenty miles of concrete sidewalks. A labor shortage prompted the company to recruit workers from central and eastern Europe, and by 1930 the still unincorporated town numbered about 6,000 inhabitants. "During the 1920s Lynch was a coal town demonstrating both enlightened paternalism and company domination," historian Thomas A. Kelemen concluded. The city "could lay little claim to being an ideal community, but it could make a strong case in the 1920s for being the greatest coal town in the world."

The great Appalachian iron and coal town boom of 1889–1893 intensified the pace of urbanization in the southeastern section of Kentucky and reflected the optimism and exuberance of the age. During this brief period more than 125 cities were promoted throughout the Appalachian region. A correspondent of the *New York Herald* proclaimed in 1890 that "from Roanoke, through Southwest Virginia, to Birmingham, Alabama, a wave of speculation is rolling, white capped with the dollars of the rich and the poor.... Dazzling, bewildered excitement is everywhere. Where the cannons boomed in the sixties, dollars are rattling now. Towns are founded here with a rapidity and ease that is simply astonishing." Another observer stated that "towns which were obscure little villages ten years ago, have become cities, counting their inhabitants by the thousands and tens of thousands." There was talk of "a law of accelerating demand" for iron products, and there was the "wildest plunging" in "brand new towns or cities yet to be established." A reporter for the *New York Herald-Tribune* tried to convey the amazingly buoyant spirit of the boom in 1890. "It impregnates the air, the earth—is omnipresent," he shouted. "It is gluttonous, rapacious, insatiable. It permeates your clothing, gets into your pockets, tickles your ribs, deafens your ears, flies into your mouth."

The Appalachian region of eastern Kentucky was hailed as a land of "inexhaustible wealth" destined to become "a luminous spot in some bright chapter in our country's history." In November 1888 the editor of the London *Mountain Echo* declared that "this section of Kentucky is destined at no distant date to become the richest part of the state." A *Courier-Journal* correspondent wrote that "this land of hills is a land of wonderful resources, and the day will come when it will hold its head with the wealthiest regions." The editor of the *Hazel Green Herald* proclaimed in 1893 that "while the mountains of Eastern Kentucky are now in a position that they 'never get nothing no how' by reason of the selfishness of the other sections, the time is fast approaching when the balance of the state must kneel at the feet of these same mountains and beg favors. We hardly hope to realize this state of affairs, but the younger generation now coming on will be the autocrats and that part of the state east of Winchester will have both the population and the wealth. That time is as sure to come as taxation and death."

The greatest boom town in the Kentucky mountains was Middlesboro, transformed from a tiny hamlet into a bustling city almost overnight. Hailed as "the Magic City of the Mountains," "the Queen of Them All," and "the Pittsburgh of the South," the city was planned by Scottish investor Alexander Arthur, who toured the area in 1886 and envisioned another industrial Midlands in the lovely Yellow Creek Valley. Returning to England, Arthur formed the American Association Limited in 1887 and secured a reported $10 million in financial backing. He then went back to Kentucky to lay out the projected "Anglo-American metropolis" he named Middlesborough. In early 1888 work was begun on a railroad to Knoxville, a tunnel to run under the Cumberland Gap, and a branch of the L&N from Corbin south to the new community. Coal and iron mines were opened, coke ovens built, steel mills and blast furnaces erected, and other industries established. A tent city sprang up, and almost as quickly wooden structures replaced the canvas shelters. Speculative fever ran high, with twenty-five-foot-wide lots bringing $250 to $350 a front foot by 1890. A single great land sale netted more than $700,000. "Who has anything on Cumberland Avenue?" anxious investors asked one another. "What have you got on Petersburg?" "How much on Avondale and the Oval?" "How's lots?" By 1890 the city contained half a dozen churches, a public library, an opera house, a golf course, and a sumptuous hotel which was built "with money being no consideration on its beautiful decorations and ornaments." Estimates of the size of the city at the height of the boom ran as high as 17,000, and boosters claimed that the community's population would reach 100,000 by 1900. Enthusiastic local businessmen boasted that "instead of a boom or mushroom city . . . we have in Middlesborough a model city, built upon the most modern and substantial plans and ideas, and a city designed more as a metropolis as aught else."

In 1890, however, a calamitous fire tore through the heart of Middlesboro's central business district. The failure of the Baring Brothers Bank of London that same year jolted the American Association, caused the value of individual shares in the company to plummet from £40 to £1.5 in less than six months, and led to the dismissal of Alexander Arthur for mismanagement and incompetence. The panic of 1893 totally destroyed the already weakened enterprise. Banks failed, mines closed, giant iron furnaces shut down, and stores boarded up their doors. The Middlesborough Town Company auctioned off all of its properties, and the American Association mortgaged 70,000 acres of land to a New York bank. On October 27, 1893, at an extraordinary general meeting of the American Association in London, shareholders passed a resolution declaring bankruptcy. In 1900 census officials could find only 4,162 people in the town, and a Middlesboro journalist suggested that "it may be doubted if ever in the history of 'boom' towns there had been so complete a collapse."

When the promoters of tiny Glasgow, Virginia, declared in 1890 that "the history of Middlesborough, Kentucky, is to be repeated," they did not realize how accurate and ironic their prediction would become. For the great boom was inevitably followed by the great bust. The nonexistent paper towns promoted by unscrupulous land sharks never got started in the first place. Once-hopeful speculative ventures declined as thin beds of low quality iron or coal ore were played out. Other struggling communities could not survive the acute economic depression which followed the financial panic of 1893. Land prices fell sharply, mining camps shut down, and "instant cities" vanished. Only a tiny fraction of the mining communities ever developed the diversified economic foundations necessary to sustain significant and long-term urban growth. In general, nearby established commercial or industrial centers benefitted the most from the mining of coal and iron, and provided marketing, banking, and other urban services to the mining districts. The very topography of the mountains militated against the growth of large cities, cutting off access to tributary hinterlands and severely limiting stretches of level land suitable for expansion. The only substantial communities in the Appalachian region of Kentucky—Ashland and Catlettsburg to the north on the Ohio River and Middlesboro in the extreme southeastern corner of the state at Cumberland Gap—are located on the periphery of the mountains.

During the boom the promoters of upstart cities touted the advantages of speculative city building. "Boom towns are good things," one publicist argued in 1890. "They bring population and increase general prosperity. Let the boomers continue and give the boomer a banquet. He deserves it." Another editor suggested, in the true spirit of the New South, that "the man who builds a factory and furnishes employment for labor . . . is the South's greatest benefactor." Boosters pointed to Birmingham and to such successful western cities as Chicago, Kansas City, and Wichita to support the claims that their own promotional ventures would inevitably flourish. The developers dismissed critics of

Cumberland Avenue, Middlesboro, looking toward "The Gap,"
May 1890

The Louisville Booster Car, 1927

boosterism as "kickers" and "knockers." One contemptuous editor maintained that "after God had finished the Rattlesnake, the Toad and the Vampire, he had some awful substance left, from which he made the Knocker. A Knocker is a two-legged animal with a corkscrew soul [and] a water sogged brain. . . . When he comes down the street honest men turn their backs; the angels in heaven shed tears and Satan shuts the gates of Hell, to keep him out."

Most of the knockers, who added a few sour notes to the otherwise harmonious fanfare of the promotional horn tooters, represented the larger and well-established older cities. Henry Watterson, editor of Louisville's *Courier-Journal,* denounced booms in general and warned that "the 'boom' is the devil's own invention, first to rob the victim of his money and then the 'boomer' of his soul. Cities are not built by 'booms.' They are the merest artificial stimulants, compounded of brandy, printer's ink and midnight, and as fatal to the community to which they are applied as a dynamite shell." Another critic claimed that "the price of over two hundred dollars a front foot for mud a foot deep, and as likely to become town property as a lot in the desert of Sahara, is sufficient evidence of the lunacy of the purchasers." Yet another kicker sneered that "land which cost a few dollars per acre is cut up into lots and sold for thousands. Then the boomer looks out for fields that are new, pastures that are green, and suckers that are fresh. . . . There are booms and booms and boomerangs." Even the editor of the *Middlesborough News* complained at the height of the boom of the "mass of advertisements of land sales in various parts of the country. . . . One almost becomes nauseated with the thought of corner lots."

After the turn of the century, a discernible shift in the character of urban promotional activities took place. Almost all of the localities destined to become major cities had already been founded, and the urban network in Kentucky, as in the nation as a whole, had been largely completed. During the formative period boosters had sought to secure transportation connections and to foster commercial enterprise in struggling young communities. In the twentieth century promoters labored to attract manufactures and industry to already well-established centers. After 1900 developers tended to set up more elaborate and complex promotional organizations, and municipal governments began to take over the management of development programs from private business groups. Communities offered a wider and more varied range of inducements to attract outside investors, including tax concessions, formalized local investment plans, comprehensive loan programs, and industrial parks. In place of the old "hot air" boosterism in which every aspect of the locality was applauded, development agencies began to publish detailed statistical reports which included data on land and plant availability, sources of raw materials, transportation, utility services, markets, living costs, housing, education, recreational facilities, and cultural amenities.

In the early years of the twentieth century, American cities began to work out systematic industrial development plans which featured the use of formally constituted industrial development corporations. One of the earliest and most widely known of these was the quasi-public Louisville Industrial Foundation, established in 1916 at a time when local business conditions were seriously depressed and workers were moving away to more promising localities. Louisville civic leaders organized a drive for a "Million-Dollar Factory Fund" which would be placed under the control of a privately owned and managed corporation. The chief purpose of this corporation would be the economic advancement of the Louisville area through industrial development. Through enthusiastically worded newspaper articles, pamphlets, and speeches, business leaders appealed to both enlightened self-interest and civic patriotism. One "pep" leaflet shouted "COMPATRIOTS! Louisville's psychic hour booms! The tragic question is: Charge or Retreat? Our future chance is a bid for action!" The organizers achieved their goal in a mere eleven days. The articles of incorporation of the nonprofit Louisville Industrial Foundation revealed a combination of private business characteristics and quasi-public motives, proclaiming that "the nature of its business shall be to advance and develop the City of Louisville and vicinity industrially." The foundation served as a kind of industrial bureau, collecting and distributing information and data concerning the Louisville area, compiling reliable briefs on land sites suitable for manufacturing concerns, and answering business inquiries. It used its funds to make low-interest medium-term loans to manufacturers who could not obtain "the equivalent amount of capital on comparable terms" elsewhere, to be used to construct or enlarge plants and to purchase or modernize mechanical equipment. By operating a revolving loan fund, the foundation was able to reuse its capital to support industrial development. During its first three decades the foundation succeeded in attracting almost fifty manufacturing enterprises whose combined operations greatly expanded the economy of the city. The Louisville Industrial Foundation, economist Ernest J. Hopkins concluded, performed "a strategic role in rounding out and supplementing Louisville's structure of organized finance."

Despite the new emphasis on such technical aspects of urban promotion as precise data and specialized information, traces of the old booster enthusiasm could still be found in promotional efforts. In the spring of 1927, for example, three Louisville promoters made a 3,000-mile roundabout trip in a shiny white Model T Ford touring car called the Louisville Booster Car. The purpose of their journey was to let people know that Louisville had become the "premier industrial location of America." One side of their car carried the exaggerated message that Louisville's population had jumped 48 percent since 1920, from 234,891 to 347,774, while a silver spare-tire cover bore the inscription "Fastest Growing City in the South." The boosters carried letters and pamphlets from Mayor Arthur Will to the mayors of the cities on the tour, inviting them to visit the Falls City and "enjoy true Kentucky hospitality." In two weeks the promoters visited over sixty cities, including Dayton, Cincinnati, Milwaukee, Detroit, Chicago, Philadelphia, Atlantic City, Syracuse, Boston, and New York. In Manhattan the Louisvillians were greeted by Mayor Jimmy Walker and their automobile "purred over the streets of Gotham gleaming from a vigorous polishing." Everywhere the boosters stopped they attracted crowds of curious onlookers, in part because, as a reporter noted, "these messengers of goodwill wore apparel in harmony with the eye-arresting glamour of their car—white flannel knickers and caps, red-checked golf hose, patterned sweaters, and white belted motoring coats embroidered on the back in red silk 'From My Kentucky Home.'" Upon their return to Louisville, the boosters were greeted by a fire department band and triumphantly paraded down the main thoroughfare of the city.

5

SEGREGATION AND SOCIAL CONTROL

COMIC song-and-dance man Thomas D. Rice came to Louisville for the 1828–1829 theatrical season as a member of Samuel Drake's illustrious touring company. At a stable located near Drake's City Theatre, Rice observed the movements of an elderly slave named Jim Crow, described by contemporary Noah Ludlow as "a very black, clumsy negro." As the slave tended his chores, he shuffled about, singing a little tune and, on the refrain, executing an awkward jump. Rice decided to incorporate the slave's mannerisms into a blackface routine designated in the theater's program as "the comic Negro song of 'Jim Crow.'" Outfitted in tattered clothing, Rice strode the boards, grinning broadly and singing:

> First on de heel tap, den on de toe,
> Ebery time I wheel about I jump Jim Crow.
> Wheel about an' turn about an' do jis so,
> An' ebery time I wheel about I jump Jim Crow.

The Louisville audience went "wild with delight," demanding encore after encore of the routine. When Rice made his New York debut in 1832, the patrons called him back at least twenty times to repeat "his celebrated song of Jim Crow." Rice became the first blackface comedian in theatrical history to be featured in his own act, and he would later be acknowledged as the "father of American minstrelsy." For almost a decade he was the greatest drawing card on the American theater circuit, as audiences clamored for performances of blackface comedy, song, and dance. To these white audiences, Jim Crow represented the reassuring stereotype of the Negro: guileless and childlike, irrepressible and uninhibited, happy and contented.

Subsequent generations of Americans would recognize the name Jim Crow as the designation for an entire system of race relations based upon segregation. It was particularly significant in this regard that Rice originated the minstrel character Jim Crow in the city, rather than on the farm or the plantation. For segregation as a method of social control also originated in the city, and was developed to meet peculiarly urban needs. In Louisville as in cities throughout Dixie, the "peculiar institution" of slavery broke down. The network of restraints so effective in isolated rural settings proved far less effective in the volatile world of the city. As the chains of slavery weakened, anxious whites in antebellum cities devised an elaborate system of segregation to govern relations between the races and to reimpose order and control.

On the eve of the Civil War, slavery was disintegrating in the cities of Kentucky and the South. In Louisville slaves comprised less than 10 percent of the total population in 1860, and during the preceding decade the number of bondsmen had declined from 5,432 to 4,903. Forty years earlier, by contrast, the system had seemed as viable in the city as on the plantation. In 1820 slaves constituted more than one-fourth of Louisville's entire population, and over 50 percent of the city's white inhabitants owned one or more slaves. Bondsmen performed nearly all of the unskilled and menial labor in southern cities. They built the municipal installations, handled most domestic chores, and worked in factories, warehouses, and shops. Slaves served as carters, porters, hack drivers, general handymen, stevedores, grave diggers, bootblacks, servants, cooks, waiters, laundresses, and domestics. "Almost all of the labor is performed by slaves," traveler James McBride remarked while visiting early Lexington. "They are the only waiters, and very few of the white people can wait upon themselves in the smallest matter." Slavery declined in southern cities not because it proved economically inefficient or unprofitable, but rather because characteristics inherent in urban life weakened the traditional foundations and structure of the "peculiar institution" and transformed the slaves themselves in ways white southerners found objectionable.

Contemporary observers recognized that urban slaves differed from their country cousins. Even before 1800, a visitor described country slaves as "contented, sober, modest, humble, civil and obliging," in contrast to their urban counterparts, whom he found "rude, unmannerly, insolent, and shameless." In 1835 the editor of the *Louisville Public Advertiser* complained that "negroes scarcely realize the fact that they are slaves [in the city]. They become insolent, intractable, and in many instances wholly worthless. They make free negroes their associates, and imbibe feelings and imitate their conduct, and are active in prompting others to neglect their duty and to commit crime." The distinctions between rural and urban slaves were so noticeable that even mid-nineteenth-century vaudeville reflected them. Jim Crow competed for audience attention with city-bred Zip Coon, a stylishly outfitted, strutting dandy from Broadway who claimed to be a "larned skolar."

Some observers maintained that the very fabric of urban life undermined the system of servitude. John S.C. Abbott, a sympathetic northern traveler, stated in 1859 that "the atmosphere of the city is too life-giving, and creates thought. . . . The city, with its intelligence and enterprise, is a dangerous place for the slave. He acquires knowledge of human rights, by working with others who receive wages when he receives none; who can come and go at their pleasure, when he from the cradle to the grave must obey a master's imperious will. . . . It is found expedient, almost necessary, to remove the slave from these influences, and send him back to the intellectual stagnation and gloom of the plantation." One southerner told Abbott bluntly that "the city is no place for niggers. They get strange notions in their heads, and grow discontented. They ought, everyone of them, be sent back on to the plantations." A Falls City observer reported in 1848 that "slavery exists in Louisville . . . only in name, [for] there are two things that always, and under all circumstances, abrogate slavery. The first is a dense population, . . . the next [is] the intelligence of slaves. Both of these are silently and imperceptibly working their legitimate results." Frederick Law Olmsted similarly concluded that "slaves can never be brought together in denser communities but their intelligence will be increased to a degree dangerous to those who enjoy the benefit of their labor."

As urban life gradually transformed slavery, the white residents of southern cities expressed increasing concern and alarm. "The evil lies," a committee of worried urban residents concluded in 1859, "in the breaking down [of] the relation between master and slave—the removal of the slave from the master's discipline and control, and the assumption of freedom and independence on the part of the slave, the idleness, disorders, and crime which are consequential." Since few owners could profitably employ all their hands, slaves were allowed to hire their own time, paying their owners a percentage of their earnings. These bondsmen were frequently permitted to live away from their master's residence as well. Concerned citizens constantly urged municipal authorities to tighten the control over slaves. As early as 1800, "numerous complaints" reached Lexington's trustees about slaves "being permitted to hire themselves, and keep houses that disturb the peace and quiet of society." One Louisvillian grumbled that "those who hire their own time, not only act without restraint themselves, but their example induces others to believe that they can take the same liberties . . . ; that they can work or play as they please." Owners could not prevent slaves from congregating with free blacks and with whites in the workplace, in back streets and alleys, in rented rooms and out-of-the-way houses, in churches and grog shops. "Free persons of color," described by one southerner as occupying "a sort of uncertain and undefined position in our midst," gravitated to the cities and became proportionately the most highly urbanized group in the Old South. One Louisville official in 1829 labeled the freedmen "an unprofitable and dangerous part of the population," and municipalities passed ordinances condemning contacts between free blacks and hired-out slaves as threats to racial order. In 1851 the editor of the *Louisville Daily Democrat* expressed the widely held opinion that "the free negro question is the most insoluble of all the social problems of the day, and stands as a practical sarcasm on all the theories of abolition and emancipation."

White residents of southern cities sought to maintain discipline and dominance by selling off young Negro males to rural plantations and by tightening emancipation procedures. In addition, and most importantly, they developed a new and intricate system of racial deference more appropriate to urban life than traditional slavery. This new system embodied most of the features that would later be identified as segregation. As historian Richard C. Wade noted, "segregation sorted people out by race, established a public etiquette for their conduct, and created social distance where there was physical proximity. . . . Increasingly public policy tried to separate the races whenever the surveillance of the master was likely to be missing. To do this, the distinction between slave and free Negro was erased; race became more important than legal status; and a pattern of segregation emerged inside the broader framework of the 'peculiar institution.'"

Under the new arrangement, blacks both slave and free were excluded entirely from public accommodations or were restricted to separate and generally inferior facilities. Taverns, restaurants, hotels, and public grounds were always off-limits to Negroes. Cultural and recreational establishments segregated the races when they did not exclude blacks altogether. Similarly, white and black were kept apart in jails, poor houses, hospitals, and cemeteries. When Karl Bernhard visited Louisville in 1825 he found the city's most important hospital facilities to have "roomy and well aired apartments for the white patients, and in the basement, those for the negroes and coloured persons." Practices regarding specific institutions differed from city to city, and no community could ever bring about the complete separation of the races. But segregation was everywhere extensive enough to serve as a constant reminder to blacks of their inferior position.

The Civil War intensified the problem of race relations in southern cities by eliminating the last vestiges of human chattel slavery. The editor of the *Daily Louisville Democrat* confessed in 1865 that "this Negro question is a much greater puzzle than the slavery question." Freedmen flocked to the cities as havens from the insecurities and isolation of plantation life and as centers of educational and occupational opportunity. Louisville's black population jumped from 6,810 in 1860 to 14,956 a decade later, an increase of 120 percent. During each of the last three decades of the nineteenth century the Falls City's black population rose by at least 35 percent. By 1900 the Negro population of the city stood at 39,139, and nearly one out of every five Louisvillians was black. This influx of blacks and the resultant problem of social control greatly troubled whites. In their view the Negroes "infested" the cities, "clogged" the streets, and threatened the restoration of peace and prosperity.

The postwar urban race crisis in the South was resolved by widening and tightening the system of segregation. White urban southerners at first attempted to exclude blacks from urban services and public accommodations entirely. When exclusion failed, they imposed an elaborate system of rigid segregation, sanctioned by custom, public policy, and law. After 1890, at the state level, Jim Crow laws ratified the policies of segregation already firmly entrenched in the cities and transformed *de facto* arrangements into *de jure* ones. The Supreme Court's 1896 ruling in the case of *Plessy* v. *Ferguson* established the "separate but equal" principle as the law of the land. In the cities, facilities had been separate since before the Civil War, and they had also been invariably unequal.

Between 1865 and 1890, the system of segregation in Louisville was extended and elaborated. The police force, fire department, city jail, hospitals, and work house all were segregated. The passenger depot of the Louisville and Nashville Railroad separated the races in waiting rooms and lavatories, and on the trains themselves blacks were not seated in first-class coaches even when they held first-class tickets. The Opera House and the Masonic Temple reserved special sections for Negroes, and there were "negro bars," "negro billiard rooms," and "resorts for ebony-colored gentlemen." In 1869 the editor of the *Courier-Journal* complained that blacks were attempting to thrust themselves on whites in certain hotels and on steamboats where they were manifestly unwelcome. "Some negroes know their place, and some do not," he insisted, "and those that do not will always be numerous enough to make themselves a disgusting nuisance."

The city of Louisville provided separate buildings for the "indigent colored population" in 1869, on the recommendation of the attending physicians. "As the political status of the black is now changed, and some provision must be made for their sick and poor, we suggest that cottages be erected on the Alms-House grounds for any future applicants for the city's charity," the doctors advised municipal authorities. "As it now is, if the keeper of the Alms-House is compelled to receive them, there is no alternative but to place them in the same building with the whites. This is objectionable, and should be attended to in time." City authorities attended to it at once, and a group being shown the premises in 1870 reported merrily that in "the apartments for negroes . . . may be found some jolly old remnants of the slave times."

In 1875 the General Council appropriated funds to erect a separate building on the grounds of Louisville's House of Refuge for "uncontrollable colored boys, who, though vicious, are yet too young to send to the Work House or Penitentiary." The white and Negro youngsters were kept apart at all times, except perhaps while at work in the greenhouse. Blacks were not permitted to work with whites in the shoe-shop, engine room, or cane-seating shop. In 1881, when colored youngsters were put to work in the cane-seating shop, white youths were no longer employed there. The boys ate in separate dining rooms, studied with separate teachers in separate classrooms, and slept in separate dormitories. Even a proposed library was to have separate branches for each race. "A library in each department is very much needed," an official advised the General Council in 1879. "I would therefore ask the privilege of purchasing about two hundred volumes for the [white] boys . . . and about one hundred for the colored children as a nucleus or a beginning. These books of course must be carefully selected." It was never suggested that Negro boys occupy the same facility as the white boys, even though authorities recognized that maintaining segregated facilities "makes the duties more exacting and laborious, both upon the physician and the general care-takers."

Louisville established a system of education for black children in 1871, designed to be completely separate from its white counterpart. The city's new charter provided that "neither the General Council of the city of Louisville nor the Board of Trustees of said schools shall suffer children of the African race to become pupils of said schools with white children." Louisvillians took pride in their accomplishments in education, but were so concerned about racial matters that it proved difficult to find a suitable location for the first Negro school. "There is no little anxiety manifested by the people living in this district in regard to locating this school," the *Courier-Journal* reported. "One great objection urged against some of the bids is the close proximity of the property offered to the Seventh ward school. Persons of all political opinions who send their children to school on the corner of Fifth and York streets, object to this school being anywhere near that school house, on the ground that it will either be a practical mixing of the children or the boys of the two schools will be continually fighting."

Every community contrived the separation of the races in most areas of daily life, but specific arrangements differed from city to city and there were always exceptions to the general pattern. In Louisville, as the *Courier-Journal* reported in 1870, there was "a preconcerted attempt to test the legal right of the city railway corporations to forbid the riding of negroes or colored men upon their cars." Two blacks filed suit against the Central Passenger Railroad Company in the United States District Court, and in May 1871 Judge Bland Ballard ruled that chartered companies could not designate what class or race of citizens they would transport. Fear of federal intervention produced sullen local compliance with the ruling, and Louisville streetcars remained desegregated from that point on. But the editor of the *Courier-Journal* warned his readers in the aftermath of the streetcar incident that "the conflict which extremism has brought is serious and bodes danger. Its practical solution seems to us to be for the present the complete separation of the two races, giving to each its share in the common lot. The blacks have their place at the theater. They have their churches. They should have their schools and their railway carriages and their street cars and their department at the hotels. . . .

This appears to be the only feasible outlet to our present complications. The races do not desire to be huddled together, and cannot be safely huddled together."

Although the races could never be said to have "huddled together," whites and Negroes did live in closer proximity during the early nineteenth century than they would in later decades. In the 1820s and 1830s blacks were widely dispersed throughout the metropolises of Dixie. Slaves usually lived behind their masters' houses in cabins facing alleyways lined with the shacks of other slaves and free blacks. Negro housing was not geographically segregated in antebellum southern cities, and the typical pattern provided for a virtual mixture of white and black in each section of town. In Louisville, the assessment books of 1834 reveal that each of the city's five wards, except the fifth, was about half Negro. Jegli's city directory of 1845 listed Louisville's population by race and ward and disclosed the absence of residential segregation or even of significant Negro concentrations. An important purpose of this residential mixture was to keep blacks divided and thereby prevent the development of a cohesive Negro society.

By the 1840s and 1850s, a measure of residential segregation had begun to appear in southern cities. As the system of slavery weakened, bondsmen drifted away from their masters' homes and found new lodgings along with free Negroes in shantytown settlements on the outskirts of the cities, as far away from white surveillance as it was possible for them to get. There was not full residential segregation—few neighborhoods, blocks, or streets became solidly black—but clusters of Negroes began to emerge on the fringes of the cities. During the immediate post-Civil War period, this trend toward clustering became more pronounced.

After 1880, although residential segregation continued to increase, whites began to move outward to the suburban periphery while blacks moved back toward the center of town and concentrated in what grew to become inner-city ghettoes. This redistribution of the races occurred in part because revolutionary developments in mass transportation shattered the boundaries of the compact "walking cities" and enabled white inhabitants with means to move out to quieter, cleaner, and less congested "streetcar suburbs." A changing occupational structure, moreover, meant that more blacks began to be employed in tasks other than working in the homes of whites. An acute housing shortage during a period of extraordinary urban expansion, militant white racism, and a desire among blacks to live near family and friends reinforced the concentration of Negroes in downtown neighborhoods. By the 1890s Louisville's black ghetto was developing in two sections along the eastern and western flanks of the central business district, and heavily black areas with nicknames such as "Smoketown" and "Little Africa" had emerged. An analysis of the federal census ward figures indicated that between 1870 and 1920 there was a progressive increase in the index of residential segregation in Louisville, as in other southern cities. In 1870, for example, the Falls City's tenth ward was 20 percent black, with 2,255 Negroes and 9,161 whites. Fifty years later the ward had become 69 percent black, with 8,385 Negroes and only 3,784 whites.

As with most other aspects of urban life, the housing blacks inhabited was both increasingly separate and decidedly unequal. Investigator Janet E. Kemp, author of the 1909 *Report of the Tenement House Commission of Louisville,* reported that poor blacks lived in "peculiarly depressing" conditions in basement dwellings that were "very poorly lighted and ventilated," and in tenement houses originally constructed for single families but redesigned to accommodate from two to eight families. The "Tin House"—described as "a large colored tenement . . . built of wood, but sheathed in tin"—housed thirty-one families in thirty-seven rooms "that are less attractive, less clean, less wholesome than many stables." The tenants were provided with "sanitary accommodations that can only be described as revolting and indecent, and which contaminate every breath of air that is drawn by the tenants in the rear apartments." These "sanitary accommodations" consisted of "four ill-kept privy compartments over one common vault which was full to overflowing" and a "leaking yard hydrant" located a distance of 135 feet from the apartments in the front of the house. The commission, nevertheless, found cause for optimism. "The negroes take such conditions with a sort of come-day-go-day, happy-go-lucky philosophy, and make merry at their discomforts," Kemp reported. In 1928, Thomas Jackson Woofter,

Louisville's black ghetto, 1909: "Buzzards' Roost"

Jr., and his colleagues concluded in their study of *Negro Problems in Cities* that in Louisville black families "live in houses not fit for work animals [and] children are familiar with vice before they start to school." By that date the central city ghetto had fully emerged, giving a concrete, physical dimension to a now complete and pervasive system of segregation.

At the close of World War II, although blacks had achieved important victories in the courts and had significantly improved their economic status, the pattern of segregation and discrimination remained largely intact in Louisville and in cities throughout the South. Law and custom required that Negroes be born in segregated hospitals, attend segregated schools and churches, live in segregated neighborhoods, eat in segregated restaurants, watch movies in segregated theaters, play in segregated parks, and, after death, be buried in segregated cemeteries. Kentucky's Day Law, sponsored in 1904 by state representative Carl Day, required the physical separation of Negro and white students at all levels of public and private education, and further decreed that "no textbook issued or distributed under this act to a white school child shall ever be reissued or redistributed to a colored school child," and vice versa. Racial patterns in Louisville differed little from those of the cities of the deep South, with the exceptions that public transit facilities had been desegregated since 1871 and that blacks could vote without hindrance and had gained a foothold in public office.

Between 1945 and 1965, a largely Negro-led middle class movement, fired by the conviction that change had become both possible and necessary, set out to topple the entire edifice of officially sanctioned segregation and discrimination. Through legal action and direct action protests blacks hammered away at the system of Jim Crow with a determination and a moral fervor which brought victory in one arena after another. In 1949, Louisville history teacher and civil rights activist Lyman T. Johnson, working with the National Association for the Advancement of Colored People, brought suit against the University of Kentucky to gain admission to the graduate school. The federal court, on the basis of the "separate but equal" doctrine, ordered the University of Kentucky to admit blacks to its graduate school and to its colleges of law, engineering, and pharmacy because the Negro colleges in the state did not offer courses in these areas. This decision forced the Kentucky legislature to amend the Day Law, allowing blacks to enroll in any institution of higher learning provided that the governing body of that institution approved and that a comparable course of study was not offered at the black colleges. In 1950 and 1951, Louisville's Roman Catholic colleges, the Southern Baptist and Presbyterian theological seminaries, and the University of Louisville, all opened their doors to Negro students. The Louisville Free Public Library, which had opened its main branch to Negroes in 1948, desegregated all of its neighborhood branches in 1952. Other breakthroughs came in the city's police and fire departments and in the nursing schools of local hospitals. Louisville Negroes gained admission to the local medical society and the bar association, and enforced segregation at the Greyhound Bus Terminal came to an end. In 1954 the mayor of Louisville announced that thenceforward all civil service positions in city departments and agencies would be filled on the basis of merit without regard to race.

None of these advances came easily or without struggle. In 1947, when four Negro ministers asked the mayor of Louisville to desegregate the city's parks, the mayor told them that he would "not take the responsibility for setting a precedent which, I am convinced, would touch off a race riot. Compared to other cities Louisville has had exceptionally good race relations. The colored people of this community have their own Chickasaw Park. If I were to throw open the other parks to them, it would give the hoodlums of both races the opportunity they seek to cause trouble—trouble which would engender bitterness and hate that would take years to overcome." Law suits were introduced, and in 1951 the federal district court, declaring that it was "not a question of segregation, but of deprivation," ruled that Louisville must either let Negroes play on city golf links and fish in the park lake or else provide blacks with "separate but equal" facilities. Unable to afford the expense of building duplicate facilities, the city yielded and in 1952 opened the golf courses and the lake to Negroes. The following year the city sponsored a three-week production of *The Tall Kentuckian,* a drama about Abraham Lincoln, at the amphitheater in Iroquois Park. Since this tribute to the "Great Emancipator" was not performed in the Negro parks, blacks were admitted to the normally segregated amphitheater during the run of the play but were thereafter barred again. Negro attorneys argued in circuit court that if segregation could be suspended for three weeks there seemed to be "no reason for the rule at all any more." Blacks lost the case, but the following year the directors of the Louisville Park Theatrical Association voted to sell tickets to "anyone."

In 1954, despite these advances and after seven years of recurrent and still-pending litigation, Louisville's major parks and all of the community's swimming pools remained segregated. In early May of that year, a white baseball team from Charlestown, Indiana, came to Louisville to play a black baseball team from Central High School. Because the game was to be held in black Chickasaw Park, the director of parks refused to sanction the interracial contest and Central had to forfeit the game. Within days of this incident a unanimous Supreme Court handed down its long-awaited opinion in the case of *Brown* v.*the Board of Education of Topeka, Kansas,* overturning *Plessy* v. *Ferguson* and proclaiming that "in the field of public education, the doctrine of 'separate but equal' has no place. Separate educational facilities are inherently unequal."

On September 10, 1956, when Louisville peacefully and smoothly desegregated its public schools, the city achieved instantaneous recognition and acclaim as a "liberal" border city and a model for the rest of the nation to follow. The next morning, a front page article in the *New York Times* announced that segregation had "died quietly" in Louisville. "When the history of this proud Southern city is written, this day will undoubtedly go down as an historic landmark," the *Times'* education editor predicted. "Historians will note that a social revolution took place that may advance the cause of integration by a generation. Even in the South, it was shown here, integration can be made to work without violence." An accompanying editorial in the *Times* maintained that "Louisville is a city of many claims to fame, but no achievement so well commands the quiet satisfaction of a job well done as the orderly unexcited acceptance of desegregation within the public schools that took place there. . . . Yesterday as schools opened there were no mobs, no pickets, no need for calling the Guard to put out fires. The people of Louisville proved once again that theirs is an enlightened, civilized city, revering a great past but ready to move on with the times." The Louisville story was broadcast over the Voice of America, and people from Europe, Asia, and Africa visited the Kentucky metropolis to learn more about the city's accomplishment. Superintendent of Schools Omer Carmichael met with President Dwight D. Eisenhower at the White House, appeared on nationally televised public affairs programs, and received honorary degrees the following spring from Harvard and Yale universities, Dartmouth College, and the University of Kentucky.

Despite the accolades to this presumed "social revolution," a number of difficult problems remained to be solved in the schools. Desegregation proceeded peacefully in Louisville primarily because Carmichael's plan contained a "free choice or permissive aspect." This provision allowed parents to transfer their children to schools other than those to which they had been assigned by simply entering such a request. Almost all of the white parents whose children had been reassigned to formerly all-black schools requested and received transfers for their children to schools with little or no racial mixing. Only eighty-nine white pupils, out of a total white student population of 33,831, attended formerly all-black schools during the fall of 1956. The president of the local Parent-Teachers Association described this "permissive" feature of the plan as "a good safety valve," and Carmichael believed that without it "we would have had a great deal of trouble." The superintendent defended the provision by contending that the Supreme Court "didn't say a word about integration. It didn't order integration. It forbade compulsory segregation." The desegregation plan also stipulated that no black teachers were to be reassigned to formerly white schools. Carmichael claimed that "the average white teacher is considerably superior to the average Negro teacher in competence as a person to teach children," despite the fact that considerably more of the black teachers had earned baccalaureate and advanced college degrees than had their white counterparts. In an "exclusive interview" published in *U.S. News & World Report*, Carmichael insisted that differences in "culture" made black teachers inferior educators. "How can a person come out of a slummy, crime-ridden area of the city, with poor churches and few of the things that go to enrich life—how can a person come out of such a background the equal of one who comes out of a more cultured home in a more cultured community?" the superintendent asked. Following the desegregation of Louisville public schools in the fall of 1956, therefore, most white children attended schools staffed entirely with white teachers and integrated with but a handful of black pupils. Most of the black children attended schools staffed entirely with black instructors and integrated either not at all or with but a handful of white pupils. On September 20, 1956, the editor of the *Louisville Defender*, a black weekly newspaper, stated that "the task is not finished because less than 10 per cent of the Negro children are integrated in Louisville schools [and] Negro teachers are still relegated to mostly all-Negro schools."

If the struggle to desegregate the schools was just beginning in 1956, so also was the effort to end discrimination in public accommodations in Louisville. In that year the NAACP Youth Council planned a series of demonstrations to protest segregation in the city's downtown area. A group of young people led by Lyman Johnson marched and picketed against the policy of the dime stores to deny Negroes service at their lunch counters even though the stores depended heavily on black customers. In mid-1957, after almost six months of weekend demonstrations, the dime stores capitulated. The protesters then turned to the drugstore lunch counters, picketing for over a year without success. The struggle came to a sudden climax in December 1958 when the mayor of Kingston, Jamaica, while visiting Louisville was refused service at a Walgreen Drug Store and lodged a protest. The incident produced so much bad publicity that Walgreen's management abruptly ended all racial restrictions at its lunch counters, and the other drugstores soon followed suit.

In 1959, the Louisville chapter of the NAACP prepared to launch an all-out campaign against discrimination in downtown hotels, theaters, restaurants, and cafeterias. Large-scale demonstrations began in late 1959, focusing on the exclusionary policies

Picketers outside Louisville's Brown Theater
in December 1959

of the theaters. That holiday season, when the Brown Theater presented the motion picture version of the all-black folk opera *Porgy and Bess,* Negroes made much of the irony of their not being permitted to see the production. By late 1961, after several years of protests, an economic boycott, political wrangling, arrests, and bad publicity for the community, the city's white civic leaders concluded that segregation was ruining Louisville's progressive reputation in the field of civil rights. Accordingly, they issued a policy statement in which they put their "moral weight" behind desegregation and declared that "it is desirable that the inevitable action take place before the generally good atmosphere of the Louisville community deteriorates." On May 14, 1963, the Louisville Board of Aldermen passed a public accommodations ordinance prohibiting any place "providing food, shelter, recreation, entertainment or amusement" to the public from refusing to serve a person on the basis of race, color, religion, or national origin. The demonstrations, the economic boycott, use of the ballot to help elect less objectionable candidates, and the desire of white civic leaders to maintain the city's liberal reputation, all contributed to the final victory. Louisville's civil rights leaders recognized that the struggle for equality was far from over, but they did not let this stop them from celebrating the passage of the public accommodations ordinance the following day by going "out to dinner."

As the first city south of the Mason-Dixon line to pass a public accommodations law, Louisville once again captured the national spotlight and received much favorable publicity. The mayor of the city spoke for many of his fellow citizens in 1963 when he stated that "the stories of violence in other cities should make us proud to live in Louisville. We enjoy national prestige for sane and sensible race relations." The National Municipal League and *Look* magazine presented Louisville an All-American City Award, and the August 13, 1963, issue of *Look* carried a highly favorable article entitled "Louisville, Kentucky: The City that Integrated without Strife." The following year the Civil Rights Act barred racial discrimination in public accommodations throughout the land.

By the mid-1960s, the civil rights movement had largely succeeded in toppling the system of Jim Crow and in outlawing officially sanctioned segregation and discrimination in public facilities and accommodations. Constitutionally, blacks had become first-class citizens. They had ended decades of disfranchisement and had achieved better educational and employment opportunities. With the success of the legal quest for equality, the first stage of the modern civil rights movement had come to an end.

Louisville's Human Relations Commission, established in 1962 and one of the first such commissions in the country, conceded that vast progress had been achieved in the areas of education and public accommodations. But it maintained that problems relating to housing and employment were still largely unsolved because "these areas are much more complex and confront long-established customs based on a heritage of prejudice." The following year Louisville journalist Hunter S. Thompson published an article entitled "A Southern City with Northern Problems." Thompson suggested that "what is apparent in Louisville is that the Negro has won a few crucial battles, but instead of making the breakthrough he expected, he has come up against segregation's second front, where the problems are not mobs and unjust laws but customs and traditions. . . . The white power structure has given way in the public sector, only to entrench itself more firmly in the private. And the Negro—especially the educated Negro—feels that his victories are hollow and his 'progress' is something he reads about in the newspapers. The outlook for Louisville's Negroes may have improved from 'separate but equal' to 'equal but separate.' But it still leaves a good deal to be desired." In the same year Lyman Johnson warned that Louisville was undergoing an unwholesome transformation. "The affluent white people are moving out of town," he declared, "leaving Louisville to the Negroes and the poor whites." The more than 400 race riots that erupted in American cities during the "long, hot summers" from 1964 through 1968 dramatized the depths of black frustration, despair, and rage. The distance separating affluent, suburban whites from poverty-stricken, inner-city blacks seemed to be widening. In 1968 the National Advisory Commission on Civil Disorders, known as the Kerner Commission, gloomily reported that "our nation is moving toward two societies, one black, one white—separate and unequal."

"White flight" to the suburbs contributed to the "resegregation" of the Louisville public schools. Between 1956 and 1965, the number of students attending desegregated schools had increased each year. By 1965, 20 percent of the city's pupils were attending schools in which neither race constituted two-thirds of the total enrollment. Beginning in 1965, however, there was a reversal of this trend. By 1970 more than 95 percent of the students in Louisville attended schools in which one race predominated. In the early 1970s, Louisville and surrounding Jefferson County were found to be in violation of federal school desegregation standards. In the spring of 1975 the city and county systems merged to become the Jefferson County School System. In July of that year a federal district court, implementing a 1974 appellate court decision, ordered the community to initiate a metropolitan-area-wide, cross-district busing program for the purpose of bringing about school desegregation. Louisville was the first major city in the nation ordered to carry out such a plan. Following the *Brown* decision in 1954, Louisville's public school districts had acted to fulfill the new legal requirements "with all deliberate speed" and without specific court decrees. Twenty years later the city's public school districts resisted federal court orders every step of the way. As classes began in the fall of 1975, thousands marched in antibusing demonstrations which in places turned so violent and ugly that state troopers and National Guardsmen had to come in to help local police restore order. Louisville and its schools once again made national headlines, but this time the publicity was decidedly unflattering. "Louisville found itself abruptly face-to-face with a community crisis—and with a violently racist image to rival that of Birmingham and Boston," Roger M. Williams declared in an article in *Saturday Review*.

At the close of the 1970s, Americans and Kentuckians, blacks and whites, could reach no consensus on the meaning of the history of race relations in the cities or on the prospects for the future. Urban historian Richard C. Wade argued that "the seventies have simply tamped down the flames while the ashes still smolder," and concluded darkly that "if we do not begin to unite the metropolis and to disperse the ghetto in the next few years, the eighties will be a decade of renewed tension and turmoil and will bear out [abolitionist] Wendell Phillips' grim prophecy of a hundred years ago: 'the time will come when our cities will strain our institutions as slavery never did.'" Louisville business consultant Katherine Peden, who served as a member of the Kerner Commission during the late 1960s, was equally pessimistic. "How much longer will we be able to have such a large segment of our society deprived of opportunities the rest have?" she asked. "If we were sitting on a powder keg ten years ago, I can't see that anything much has been done to defuse it."

Other observers, reviewing the same events, interpreted their meaning quite differently. Historian Harvard Sitkoff contended that in the field of race relations "recent changes have been so dramatic that it is difficult to recall the sense of shame and resignation so common among Afro-Americans at the start of the 1960s, especially in the South. Students, Negro and white, have largely forgotten the trauma involved in having to 'test' a public restaurant, or the worry that if you did get served a hostile waitress might have spit in your soup. Few now understand the dread of a black family setting out in 1955 to drive from Atlanta to Houston: the anxiety of being refused service by motels and gas stations; the confusion about where to purchase a cup of coffee or a hamburger. It is hard to remember that in the mid-1960s, Southern blacks were still going to jail for using a 'white' public toilet or drinking fountain, or that Negroes often could not sit where they wanted to on buses and trains. . . . In ending legal inequality and the Jim Crow caste structure, the United States has demonstrated its capacity to change. For the first time in history Americans now stand on the verge of an age in which the races have more in common than what divides them."

Louisville educator Lyman Johnson remembered the indignities and injustices of the earlier decades well. He lived through that period of extraordinary change, and helped bring that change about in Kentucky as one of the Commonwealth's most eloquent and effective champions of civil rights. In 1949 Johnson had to go to court to gain admission to the University of Kentucky; thirty years later that institution awarded him an honorary doctorate in letters. "Considering the conditions that prevailed when I first came to Louisville in 1933, and the amount of change there has been since then, I don't see why we shouldn't be optimistic about the future," Johnson declared. He believed that "everything the Negro has won in Louisville has been won by fighting. Not by violence, but by insistence." Johnson recognized that "the battle is still raging," and at the age of seventy-one, though retired, he ran for election to a term on the Jefferson County school board. He won the race, and assumed his new duties in 1978 with the intention of "raising a little hell with everything that seems slipshod and inefficient in the system." On December 7, 1980, at the dedication of a middle school renamed in Johnson's honor, former Louisville school administrator Milburn Maupin suggested that many black youngsters in Jefferson County knew little of Johnson's accomplishments in the field of civil rights. But, Maupin asserted, in part "because of him they'll go to the lunch counters of their choice, go to the universities . . . of their choice, [enter] the vocations of their choice, . . . and sit in the armchairs of their choice . . . and say 'what was the hullabaloo over Lyman Johnson about?'"

6

CRUCIBLE OF CULTURE

IN 1937, JOURNALIST George R. Leighton published an article in *Harper's Magazine* entitled "Louisville, Kentucky: An American Museum Piece." Leighton charged that Louisville had become "the city of let-well-enough-alone," and had prematurely entered upon an "ossified dotage." "That any genuine intellectual life could flourish in such an atmosphere was of course impossible," he sneered. "In the sciences there was a stygian darkness. Poetry was represented by the maunderings of Madison Cawein; the high point in the novel was *Mrs. Wiggs of the Cabbage Patch*." Anyone possessing an "active intellect was apt to move away," for all that remained of the creative vitality of the once-thriving commercial emporium was a certain "moth-eaten, moribund 'charm.'"

In 1955 writer William Manchester reassessed cultural life in the Falls City and discovered evidence of a profound metamorphosis. In an article published in *Harper's* entitled "Louisville Cashes In on Culture," Manchester drew an analogy to the world of professional golf and proclaimed that Louisville was "the Ben Hogan of American cities. It has staged a spectacular comeback, rising, in less than two decades, from stagnation to prosperity." The city's leaders, he maintained, "are convinced that [Louisville's] greatest resource is a reputation for intellectual vigor. . . . Here is the only American city which has ever used culture as an industrial asset. Louisville has succeeded where other Southern cities have failed because it has deliberately made itself a pleasant, stimulating place to live."

Contemporary observers agreed that in the brief period of eighteen years Louisville had undergone a striking transformation from ossified "museum piece" to cultural showpiece. The community's symphony orchestra, under the leadership of founder and conductor Robert S. Whitney, had spearheaded this cultural renaissance. Louisville's imaginative and eccentric mayor, Charles P. Farnsley, had developed the ideas and formulated the plans that had brought Louisville international acclaim as a "world musical center." Whitney reflected that "it was Farnsley's comprehension of the value of the fine arts in raising the 'image' of a community in the eyes of the world that made his contribution so remarkable. . . . Charlie said, 'Athens was a much smaller city than Louisville, and our city, in its own way, can go down in the history books too.'"

In 1937, the year Leighton's article appeared in *Harper's,* the Louisville Civic Arts Association set out to establish a civic orchestra. Amateur and semiprofessional orchestras had served Louisville for varying periods of time since 1822, but none had ever gained a firm foothold. The Board of Directors of the Civic Arts Association realized that in order to create a first-rate permanent orchestra they would have to secure the services of a talented conductor who possessed the proper credentials, experience, and temperament. "The man must be able to train a raw orchestra," one patron of the arts declared, "be a real musician and—terribly important—know how to meet people, go to parties, kiss hands, [and] remember dowagers." The board hired thirty-three-year-old pianist, composer, and conductor Robert Whitney to conduct and develop the semiprofessional, part-time Louisville Civic Orchestra.

In December 1947, after a decade of struggle, the orchestra's prospects were bleak. The ensemble's debt had grown annually and had surpassed $40,000. Concert audiences had become so small that the orchestra's management offered the musicians a 10 percent commission on any tickets they could sell. Local arts patrons had given generously to the Louisville Philharmonic Progress Fund to enable the orchestra to pay off its debt and establish itself on a firm financial basis. But the orchestra's Board of Directors believed that these same people would not be willing to contribute repeatedly to "bail the orchestra out." The board reluctantly concluded that if the orchestra could not earn its own way during the 1947–1948 season, the enterprise would have to be abandoned.

Early in 1948 the Louisville Philharmonic Society, which had succeeded the Civic Arts Association as the orchestra's sponsoring body, elected Charles Farnsley its president. Farnsley was something of a student of history, and had concluded that solutions to at least some twentieth-century problems could be found by studying eighteenth-century customs and traditions. He had worked out a series of changes which he believed would strengthen and revitalize the Louisville Orchestra, and he called Whitney to his office to discuss these measures with him.

The plan Farnsley outlined contained three major features. He proposed first of all that Whitney trim the number of musicians from eighty or so down to about fifty. The resulting ensemble would resemble the classical court orchestras of the eighteenth century for which Haydn and Mozart had composed their music. Farnsley argued that the smaller orchestra would provide Whitney the opportunity to weed out the weaker players, would be less expensive to maintain, and would be easier to take on tour and into broadcast studios. He next suggested that the orchestra adopt the eighteenth-century custom of presenting a new piece of music at every concert. Urging the conductor to "let concert-going be an adventure—an occasion to hear something new and challenging," Farnsley proposed that the orchestra take the money normally spent to bring in a guest soloist and use it instead to commission a new piece of music tailor-made for an orchestra of classical size. The Louisville Orchestra would then give the new work its "world premier." Finally, predicting that the long-playing records which had just been put on the market would "be as revolutionary for music as the invention of the printing press was for the written word," Farnsley proposed that the Louisville Orchestra plan to record the new works of music it commissioned. "If you follow my suggestions," Farnsley concluded, "the orchestra will be heard on the radio networks, it will record, and, if you commission a new work for each concert, the orchestra will be imitated by other orchestras and you'll be famous."

The astonished conductor found Farnsley's plan very appealing. A composer himself, Whitney believed that the work of living composers was being neglected "to the great detriment of the art" in favor of what he termed "sure-fire" music. He thought to himself that "if only 25 percent of what Farnsley predicts comes to pass, it will still be a big step forward." Whitney therefore agreed to try to implement the plan. Several days after their meeting the city's Board of Aldermen appointed Farnsley to succeed the community's recently-deceased mayor. Farnsley would not be able to retain the presidency of the Philharmonic Society, but he would be able to do more for the orchestra in his capacity as mayor of Louisville. Indeed, he wasted no time in organizing the Louisville Fund, a community chest for all the arts and the first such "umbrella" organization of its kind in the country.

When the board of the Philharmonic Society voted to continue to sponsor the orchestra during the 1948–1949 season, Whitney set about putting Farnsley's ideas into practice. The conductor reduced the size of his ensemble and began to perform his concerts in a smaller auditorium. The orchestra commissioned new works of music, invited the composers to Louisville to conduct their own compositions, and undertook to introduce a world premier at every subscription concert. Music critics from around the country began to take interest in the Louisville Orchestra's innovative programs. There were some objections raised locally to the new and frequently harsh-sounding scores, but Whitney held firm to his belief that music "is an art, not a commodity." In March 1949 Whitney informed the orchestra's directors that "much as we wish to sell more tickets to our subscription concerts we must not judge our value to the community by that criterion alone. Our true purpose is to nurture fine music in this city and build soundly for the future so that our children and grandchildren will inherit a musical tradition of excellence."

Declining attendance at the orchestra's concerts, however, precipitated another crisis. The new music had failed to attract additional subscribers and had in fact alienated many regular concertgoers. On December 23, 1949, the president of the Philharmonic Society and the president of the Louisville Fund notified Whitney that the orchestra's directors had concluded that the next pair of subscription concerts should be the ensemble's last. After January 5th the musicians would be paid and the entire debt-ridden enterprise would be "liquidated." Whitney remembered the Christmas of 1949 as "one of the darkest moments of my life."

The conductor began to work feverishly, however, for he knew that he had an extraordinary score for the upcoming concert. The orchestra had commissioned the gifted ballerina and choreographer Martha Graham to prepare a new work for the dance, and she in turn had selected one of America's foremost composers, William Schuman, to create the music. Graham chose the biblical story of Judith as her theme, and conceived a work in which a single dancer would perform as "soloist-with-orchestra." The ensemble, considered an integral part of the presentation, was seated on the stage rather than in the pit. The performance of *Judith, A Choreographic Poem* on the evening of January 4, 1950, was the turning point in the history of the Louisville Orchestra. The originality and brilliance of the concept and the superb execution of the work produced a glorious triumph. Critics from all over the country attended the premier and wrote feature stories for the major newspapers and national magazines praising the successful and popular program as well as Whitney's efforts to further the cause of new music in Louisville. Instead of closing its doors the Louisville Orchestra became famous throughout the world, and, as Whitney recalled, "no more was said about liquidating the orchestra." On December 29, 1950, the Louisville Orchestra performed *Judith* and five other works by living composers at New York City's Carnegie Hall to great acclaim. The critic of the *New York World Telegram and Sun* declared that the Louisville Orchestra "gave a program that in daring and novelty put New York's own name bands to shame." When Paul Hindemith went to Louisville that same season for the premier of his *Sinfonietta in E* he proclaimed that "what this country needs is more Louisville Orchestras."

The success of *Judith* provided the Louisville Orchestra the opportunity to put the work on a long-playing record. In September 1950 the orchestra recorded two works by William Schuman, *Judith* and *Undertow*, for the Mercury Record Corporation. Ever since record companies had begun to produce the long-playing discs in commercial quantities in 1947, Farnsley had wanted to capitalize on the new invention to promote the Louisville Orchestra. During the fall of 1952, each time the mayor went to New York City to sign city bonds, he made appointments to see officials of the Rockefeller Foundation. Farnsley gathered the necessary information and put together an ambitious grant application. On April 7, 1953, he announced that the Rockefeller Foundation had awarded the Louisville Orchestra $400,000 to be used over a four-year period to commission and record new pieces of music. The grant provided for the commissioning of forty-six new works each year, and the foundation stipulated that at least one-third of the composers had to live outside the United States. The orchestra would introduce four new works each month to local audiences at special weekly concerts, and would issue one new long-playing record each month as well. The LPs would be recorded by Columbia Records, distributed by the Louisville Philharmonic Society, sold on a yearly subscription basis, and issued to the Voice of America, Radio Free Europe, and educational radio stations at home and abroad interested in contemporary music. This grant represented the first involvement of a major national foundation with an American symphony orchestra. *Musical Journal* described the commissioning and recording project as "the most revolutionary development in contemporary musical history."

The Louisville Orchestra achieved an international reputation during the 1950s. Conductors, composers, foreign ambassadors, and music lovers throughout the world became aware of the orchestra's efforts to nurture new music and listened to its recordings. "Allow me to express the utmost admiration for your unique achievements in Louisville," Dimitri Mitropoulos, music director of the New York Philharmonic Symphony Orchestra, wrote to Whitney. "Your encouragement of contemporary music and composers has had repercussions all over the world and has . . . definitely put Louisville on the map as a world musical center." The music critic of the *Chicago Sun Times* proclaimed in December 1954 that Louisville had eclipsed such international cultural centers as New York, London, and Paris as a leader in the field of contemporary orchestral music. Three years later *Life* magazine heralded a "unique civic renaissance" taking place in "Culture's New

Kentucky Home," and declared that "Louisville is caught up in a civic cultural renaissance that is without parallel in the country."

Farnsley dreamed up other original schemes to promote the Louisville Orchestra, not all of which proved successful. At one point he suggested that the orchestra ought to play contemporary music continuously, every afternoon and evening, fifty-two weeks a year! "The motion picture theaters were his model and he wanted admission prices for these concerts to be the same as theirs," Whitney recalled. "He felt that anyone passing by at any time should be able to drop into Columbia Auditorium and, for a nominal fee, listen to contemporary music." Whitney patiently explained that he would need several orchestras and musicians with truly prodigious abilities in order to perform concerts in this marathon fashion, and he finally convinced Farnsley to abandon the idea.

Had Whitney attempted to implement Farnsley's plan, however, the conductor might well have encountered severe difficulties in persuading passersby to "drop into Columbia Auditorium." For throughout this era, angry patrons continually expressed their unhappiness over the orchestra's performances of the little understood and less appreciated unorthodox music. In February 1952 composer and guest conductor Nicolas Slonimsky led the Louisville Orchestra in an entire evening of contemporary compositions. During the third selection a prominent and exasperated local sculptor stood up, shouted "PHOOEY," and stormed out of the hall. Some in the audience followed him, and those who remained responded to the conductor and orchestra at the end of the evening by shouting and stomping their feet in disapproval. *Courier-Journal* music critic William Mootz stated that "in most respects, it was a dismal, disillusioning evening." A defender of the orchestra's policies wrote in the *Louisville Times* that "very few people limit their reading to classical literature. If they did so, they would have little conception of modern trends of thought. . . . Music is not a live art unless it is performed. If it remains on paper on the shelf it dies and our horizons close in upon us. . . . Do we want a static organization playing a limited repertory, or do we want a group of alive and alert musicians who are able to enrich our lives and broaden our appreciation?" Most

Conductor Robert S. Whitney and the Louisville Orchestra,
as depicted by artist George Joseph

Louisvillians, however, agreed with Mootz's argument that "in order to stay alive, the Louisville Orchestra must draw on a large and diversified audience.... It must satisfy the lover of Bach as well as the admirer of Bartok, capture the housewife who likes her Tchaikovsky as well as the businessman who finds his greatest source of pleasure in the melodies of Schubert."

The Slonimsky disaster discouraged everyone except the irrepressible Farnsley. "From now on we will perform just one contemporary work on each concert," he chortled, "and people will be so relieved [that] we will hear no more complaints about the matter." On March 2, 1952, the *Courier-Journal* published Whitney's response to his critics. The conductor explained that "the purpose of the commissioning policy is three-fold: to encourage the contemporary composer, to recognize the importance of the creative artist in a living art-form, and to provide for Louisville audiences the opportunity for participating in the creative musical activity of the century. I recognize the validity of the present criticism of overemphasis on contemporary music. In the future my aim will be to maintain a balance of new and novel music with great art works from the past. At the same time I also intend to present each season several solo artists of highest artistic attainment." In January 1953, with the commissioning project in its fifth season, an optimistic Whitney wrote Farnsley that "our audiences now approach our programs with an eager interest. A preconceived distaste for anything new or reflecting the spirit of our age seems to be dwindling rapidly. Our new works are no longer accepted in the spirit of tolerant resignation, but with a marked degree of anticipation and in many cases real enthusiasm." Yet disgruntled listeners continued to grumble about "the premier performances of modern din" and the "modern cacophonic programs," and one writer claimed that he subjected himself to the new music "for the same reason that the Irishman hit his thumb—'it feels so good when you stop.'" In December 1954 the *Courier-Journal*'s music critic confessed that "the truth is that, despite its international fame, the Louisville Orchestra is in much the same predicament as the prophet not without honor save in his own country."

The Rockefeller Foundation and the Louisville Orchestra had

hoped that the commissioning and recording project would become completely self-sustaining. Farnsley had predicted that 1,000 subscriptions would be registered during each of the four years under the grant, which would have generated sufficient income to continue the enterprise. He compared the monthly release of new recordings to the regular publication of scholarly and professional journals, and believed that composers, conductors, and music libraries everywhere would subscribe to the LPs. After the first year, however, only 300 subscriptions had been received, and the project never came close to enrolling the estimated 5,000 subscribers needed to make the endeavor self-supporting. The Rockefeller Foundation provided an additional $100,000 during the final year of the grant period, and in 1961 Broadcast Music Incorporated endowed the orchestra with $62,000 to commission and record new works of music. The president of BMI explained that the Louisville Orchestra was "the obvious choice [to receive the award since] it has done more for contemporary music than any other orchestra in the United States."

After 1960, although the orchestra could no longer afford to commission new works on a large scale, the ensemble continued to produce the highly regarded recordings. The number of subscriptions climbed to 2,500, a significant proportion of which belonged to universities, libraries, and schools of music which automatically entered renewals. Many of the subscriptions were held abroad, and, perhaps not surprisingly, more of the records went to subscribers in London than to purchasers in Louisville. "The recordings are extraordinarily good," the director of contemporary projects for BMI declared. "In Europe they can't believe that the Louisville group is not one of the 'majors'—one of the big city orchestras, like the Boston, the Philadelphia, or the New York Philharmonic. Of all conductors I know, Whitney has conducted more contemporary music and done it better." The Louisville Orchestra changed the name of its series from the *Commissioned Records* to the *First Edition Records*, cut the number of new releases from twelve to six per year, and remained the only orchestra in the world which recorded and distributed LPs under its own label.

Whitney strove to make the recordings representative of the new music being composed at the time. Accordingly, few of the compositions commissioned reflected extreme experimentation or innovation, and contemporary music authority Philip Hart was "impressed with the general conservatism" of the body of music. Several of the commissioned works have entered the repertory of the modern symphony orchestra and have been described by critics as masterpieces. These works include William Schuman's *Judith,* Elliott Carter's *Variations for Orchestra,* Peter Mennin's Fifth and Sixth Symphonies, Aaron Copland's *Orchestral Variations,* Walter Piston's Fifth Symphony, Roger Sessions's *Idyll of Theocritus,* and Luigi Dallapiccola's *Variazioni per Orchestra.* Overall, however, Hart concluded that "in its aggregate the Louisville First Edition repertory rather reminds one of catalogs of music in the eighteenth century, filled with composers now forgotten and only occasional mentions of such masters as Mozart and Haydn." Nevertheless, the Louisville Orchestra's recordings of hundreds of symphonic works by scores of modern composers comprise what promises to remain the most important historical introduction to the creative output of mid-twentieth-century classical music.

In 1965 Whitney and the Louisville Orchestra played the central role in the musical portion of the White House Festival of the Arts. The music critic of the *Washington Post* concluded that the conductor and his ensemble "have far outstripped every other American orchestra in their services to contemporary music in general and American music in particular. For more than a decade and a half, Louisville has commissioned works from the leading composers of the world, out of every age bracket. Moreover, they have not only performed these new scores in their regular concerts but have given them permanent form in the most distinguished series of phonograph records yet issued." At the conclusion of the 1966-1967 season, Robert Whitney retired after thirty years as conductor of the Louisville Orchestra. The ensemble continued its innovative tradition under Whitney's successor, and in 1980 the American Society of Composers, Authors, and Publishers presented the Louisville Orchestra an award for "adventuresome programming of contemporary music."

During the late 1970s, Actors Theatre of Louisville similarly gained worldwide recognition as a major force in the performing arts. The theater achieved its international reputation by doing for drama precisely what the Louisville Orchestra had done for music two decades earlier. Beginning in 1976, ATL launched a New Play Program and began to commission and produce new theatrical works. The theater sponsored an annual "Great American Play Contest" in order to discover the newest scripts written by unknown as well as established talents, and each winter mounted productions of the winning entries in its "Festival of New American Plays." At the same time ATL initiated a commissioning project which led to the development of over sixty works by American authors during the late 1970s. The theater encouraged promising playwrights by awarding them stipends and by sponsoring developmental workshops and readings. By 1980, ATL had presented the world premiers of almost fifty new plays, and the number of scripts annually reviewed by the theater's literary department had ballooned to 4,000. "We take special pleasure in discovering new writers, and working with them on their first plays," ATL's producing-director Jon Jory explained. "The theater is excited about its commitment to the playwright, a commitment of many years, and we are anxious to work with American writers at every level of their development and provide a forum for their work. . . . If we can assist new works [to] find their way into the general repertory, we're happy. We like to feel that, in the next century, some of the dramas we've introduced will still be playing around America."

In 1980, *Newsweek* magazine's drama critic reported that "the annual Festival of New American Plays at Actors Theatre of Louisville has become just about the biggest event in American regional theater. The festival has developed into an international theatrical bazaar, attracting playgoers, critics, agents and producers from all over the United States and [from] as far away as England, Italy, France, Germany, Poland, and even Australia." A surprised English theater critic remarked that same year that "there are five major British critics here [and] I don't ever remember seeing them in the same place at the same time." In 1980 the drama critic of the *London Observer* suggested that ATL's "festival of new American plays . . . is probably the most ambitious event of its kind in the English-speaking theatre." His counterpart on the *Wall Street*

Journal declared that "once a year, when the Actors Theatre of Louisville holds its Festival of New American Plays, Louisville, Kentucky, becomes the center of the American theatrical universe." The drama critic of the *Washington Post* agreed with his enthusiastic colleagues and proclaimed that "for a few days last weekend, Louisville, Kentucky, became the theater capital of the Western world."

In the space of only five years ATL achieved international acclaim and produced an impressive number of highly regarded new works. D.L. Coburn's *The Gin Game* and Beth Henley's *Crimes of the Heart* received the Pulitzer Prize for drama in 1978 and 1981, respectively, while Marsha Norman's *Getting Out* won the 1978 Outer Critics' Circle Award. The drama critic of the *Australian* recognized that "Louisville audiences liked being in at the birth of something," and Jory certainly did not have to contend with the hostility to the presentation of new works that Whitney had encountered. In fact, the theater was able to sell practically all of its tickets on a season subscription basis. Actors Theatre received the Margo Jones Award in 1978 for the discovery and production of new American plays, the Schubert Foundation's James N. Vaughan Memorial Award in 1979 for "exceptional achievement and contribution to the development and growth of professional theater," and a special American Theatre Wing Antoinette Perry Award in 1980 for outstanding theatrical achievement. No American theater had previously won all three of these prestigious awards.

During the post-World War II period American cities had become increasingly aware that the performing and visual arts could significantly enhance their prospects for economic growth. Charles Farnsley had understood this fact earlier than most. As William Manchester reported in 1955, Farnsley was "convinced that culture, industry, and retail business are woven together—that the progress of one affects the progress of the others. . . . The theory [behind his plans was] that industries which are really desirable want decent homes and cultural facilities for their employees." In the decades after 1945 cities discovered that Farnsley had been correct and that they needed to provide a broad range of cultural amenities in order to attract the "really desirable" service-based industries along with their highly trained, well educated, mobile, and salaried personnel. A 1977 *Fortune* magazine market research survey revealed that decisions involving the location of a corporate headquarters were based primarily upon the personal preferences of company executives and upon factors such as the arts which had come to be associated with a high "quality of life."

In 1978 the United States Conference of Mayors highlighted the economic importance of cultural attractions in a position paper entitled *The Taxpayers' Revolt and the Arts.* "All too often, in times of budgetary constraints, appropriations for the arts seem an unnecessary frill," Atlanta mayor Maynard Jackson wrote in the report's introduction. "We believe that money for the arts, rather than representing an unnecessary, easily cut expenditure, represents instead an investment which generates further revenues for the cities upon which future city vitality depends." Indeed, economists estimated that every dollar spent for the arts generated between three and four dollars in return, directly through salaries, the purchase of services, and the rental of buildings, and indirectly through hotel bookings, restaurant patronage, and retail sales. "As a mayor of a major urban center," Jackson declared, "I have strongly endorsed the use of the arts as a significant tool for the restoration and revitalization of the central city. . . . The arts are the very highest expression of urban life; and the cultural enrichment that is possible in an urban setting is the highest and most eloquent justification of the city itself; the arts and the city are inseparable."

7

CHANGE AND CONTINUITY

IN 1970 THE FEDERAL census revealed that, for the first time in the history of the Commonwealth, a majority of Kentuckians lived in cities. In statistical terms, 52.3 percent of the state's total population of slightly over 3.2 million lived in the 102 cities of 2,500 people or more. Kentuckians had gone to town, and although they might entertain a wistful and superficial nostalgia for "the good old days," they had no intention of returning to the land. As historian Thomas D. Clark pointed out, urban Kentuckians "love nothing better than to reminisce about those other times. They drive out on Sunday afternoons to dig through the weeds in search of familiar landmarks, to review the scenes of their childhood, and to remark on the changes, but at sundown they hustle back to town."

Throughout the twentieth century, the proportion of Kentucky's inhabitants living in cities had continued to grow, and the state's network of cities had become more extensive and complex. The Bluegrass region and its fringes experienced substantial urban development, with the rise of new suburbs outside Lexington and with the growth of places like Berea, Lancaster, and Wilmore to the south, Morehead to the east, and Lawrenceburg to the west. Older centers such as Lexington and Bardstown came to life and once again began to forge ahead. Lexington's dynamic growth during the 1960s and 1970s was stimulated by the arrival of large

Metropolitan Lexington, looking toward the southeast across downtown and the campus of the University of Kentucky

manufacturing firms such as International Business Machines, by the expansion of the University of Kentucky, and by the development of a large-scale health care industry. The city's population jumped from less than 63,000 in 1960 to more than 204,000 in 1980 as the rejuvenated "Athens of the West" surged past such cities as Des Moines, Dayton, Knoxville, and Fort Wayne and threatened to challenge Louisville for urban supremacy within the Commonwealth.

Upstart towns and cities arose and vied with economic rivals for primacy and power. Radcliff boomed after World War II as "the Post Town of Fort Knox," its population soaring from a few hundred to 15,000 as the fort developed into a permanent, major military installation. Radcliff's rapid expansion created anxiety in neighboring Elizabethtown and gave rise to a spirited urban rivalry between the two Hardin County communities. Older Elizabethtown, which billed itself "Kentucky's Hub City," was founded well before the Civil War and took pride in being a "fine, established city." But its brash young rival branded it a "very old city" to which people would move only "if they had relatives or a job there." A Radcliff booster declared that, unlike Elizabethtown, his community was "growing by leaps and bounds. People moving here can get in on the ground floor. There's room to grow." An Elizabethtown promoter smugly dismissed such claims and insisted that "it's obvious that opportunities are better here than in Radcliff."

Both Elizabethtown and Radcliff, along with dozens of other communities, benefitted from the construction of a network of roadways throughout Kentucky and from the increasing use of automobiles and trucks. The building of the Purchase, Western, and Blue Grass parkways stimulated the development of towns and cities along the routes of the new highways. The almost universal adoption of the automobile after 1945 sparked a suburban explosion on the "crabgrass frontiers" of the state's larger and older urban centers. Satellite cities developed in the northern Kentucky–Greater Cincinnati area around Covington and Newport, in the Louisville–Jefferson County area and to its south, and in the vicinity of Ashland and Paducah. Nationally, the suburban trend had become so pronounced that the 1970 federal census revealed that, for the first time in American history, more residents of metropolitan areas lived outside the central cities than within them. Kentucky's metropolitan population conformed to the national pattern, as slightly more than half of the state's metropolitan residents lived in suburban communities outside the political boundaries of the central cities.

The growth of sprawling metropolitan regions has been one of the most significant developments in the urban history of the twentieth century. By 1980, 45 percent of Kentucky's *total* population had come to reside within seven Standard Metropolitan Statistical Areas. The Census Bureau defined an SMSA as consisting of an entire county which contained a central city of 50,000 or more inhabitants, plus adjacent counties considered economically and socially integrated with the central city according to an elaborate set of criteria. Census officials ignored the somewhat arbitrary political boundaries of the states in charting the contours of metropolitan regions, and hence five of the seven SMSAs in Kentucky included portions of one or more neighboring states. The Huntington–Ashland SMSA spread over portions of West Virginia, Kentucky, and Ohio, while the Greater Cincinnati–Covington–Newport complex took in parts of Ohio, Kentucky, and Indiana. Both the Greater Louisville and the Evansville–Henderson areas straddled the Ohio River and included portions of Kentucky and Indiana, while the Clarksville–Hopkinsville region took in parts of Kentucky and Tennessee. Only the Owensboro and Lexington SMSAs lay entirely within the borders of the Commonwealth.

Rapid urban growth, suburbanization, and the rise of metropolitan areas dramatically altered the daily lives of average Americans in Kentucky as elsewhere. During the 1960s and 1970s, in the midst of a widely publicized "urban crisis," social scientists, journalists, and urban affairs commentators highlighted aspects of change and novelty in urban society and tended to ignore elements of continuity. To most observers the giant metropolis of the automobile age seemed only remotely related to the industrial city of the railroad era, the commercial emporium of the steamboat age, and the frontier community of the turnpike period. Yet a closer examination of two centuries of urban life in the nation and in the Commonwealth revealed that, despite the extraordinary amount of change, there had been a substantial although far less widely appreciated thread of continuity in the urban experience.

Noise pollution, for example, seemed to many a peculiarly modern urban problem associated principally with motorcycles, diesel trucks, power mowers, police sirens, jet aircraft, jackhammers, and rock-and-roll music. A United States Census Bureau study released in 1976 indicated that more than half of all Americans considered noise the most annoying of all contemporary urban problems. *Courier-Journal* environmental reporter Jim Detjen argued in a 1978 article headlined "Hues and Cries of Today's Life Threaten Your Sound Barrier" that "noise is more than an annoyance. It interrupts sleep, concentration and conversation. It induces stress. It causes nausea and high blood pressure. It has been linked to mental illness, sexual inhibitions, ulcers and birth defects. It also makes you deaf." Kentucky state legislator Bruce Blythe, representing Jefferson County, referred to noise as "a new kind of pollution."

Yet urban residents complained of the discomfort caused by unwanted noise long before the modern era of automobiles, airplanes, and amplifiers. Benjamin Franklin grumbled about the "thundering of coaches, chariots, chaises, wagons, drays and the whole fraternity of noise" that assailed the ears of late eighteenth-century Philadelphians. Industrialization inflicted a "diabolical symphony" of "unadulterated noise" on harried city dwellers, whose eardrums were pierced by "the whir of machinery, the shriek of whistles, the clang of bells, [and] the strident grind of trolleys." An article published in Louisville's *Courier-Journal* in 1877 revealed the extent to which noise disrupted the lives of the community's inhabitants. "Before retiring, the citizens shut down the windows, put a clothes pin upon their noses, fill their ears full of putty and then ram their heads under a pillow to keep from being awakened at midnight by pork-house whistles," the writer asserted. "The people in the East End only sleep the fore part of the night during hog-killing season. Everybody sits up from midnight till daylight cursing the inventor of steam and the son-of-a-sea-cook who invented the whistle. . . . The only good pork-house whistles do is they keep the East End police from going to sleep." Shortly after the turn of the century the chairman of the Committee on Noise of the American Civic Association insisted that, if boards of health could prevent a person "from polluting his neighbor's water-supply with typhoid germs, they can forbid him from congesting his neighbor's air with sounds that breed insanity."

In the late twentieth century, city dwellers became increasingly conscious of environmental problems and complained of the choking air pollution. "Thousands of Louisville residents dare not leave their air-conditioned homes on days when pollution is bad," *Courier-Journal* columnist John Filiatreau wrote in 1978. "People who walk around downtown complain of mysterious headaches, notice that their skin grows gummy, apologize for red, weepy eyes, suffer chest pains, find themselves short of breath." Commentators and experts blamed the automobile as the principal source of this problem. "Automotive pollutants have a stranglehold on Louisville, making its air the worst of any city in the Southeastern United States," the *Courier-Journal*'s environmental reporter declared in 1978. "Each year, Jefferson County's 384,000 cars, 62,000 trucks and 23,000 other motor vehicles spew an estimated 265,000 tons of pollutants into the air we breathe. . . . While the vehicles congest the streets, their exhausts cloud the city's economic future and endanger its citizens' health."

The air pollution problem too, however, can be traced back over the course of centuries. In 1661, for example, a fellow of the Royal Society of London named John Evelyn published *Fumifugium: Or the Inconvenience of the Aer and Smoake of London Dissipated*, a tirade against the "Hellish and dismall Cloud of SEA-COALE" and the "impure and thick Mist, accompanied with a fuliginous and filthy vapour," which caused "*Catharrs, Phthisicks, Coughs,* and *Consumptions* [to] rage more in this one City, than in the whole Earth besides." In Louisville, Henry McMurtrie complained in 1819 of "the foul and pestilent airs of a pent-up city," and Charles Dickens observed during a visit in 1842 that "the buildings are smoky and blackened, but an Englishman is well used to that appearance, and indisposed to quarrel with it." In 1849 a newcomer to the Falls City was surprised to discover that "when we put the water pitcher out the window to cool, it becomes filled with floating black particles, and the children's arms and faces are not more than fifteen minutes after washing free from soot." The increasing number of factories in the city and the widespread use of coal to heat businesses and homes produced so much smoke that a roving journalist found Louisville in 1866 considerably less charming and elegant than he had assumed it would be. "Masses of smoke, belched from numberless chimneys, keep the place in a perpetual fog, and, descending in showers of soot, produce a monotone of color not cheering to the sight," he declared. "Thus Louisville . . . turns out to be in fact only a rival of Pittsburgh." Indeed, some thought Louisville even surpassed the notorious Pennsylvania steel town in smoke and dirt. A cartoon printed in the *Courier-Journal* in 1913 entitled "Louisville's Unenviable Reputation" depicted an early model biplane flying above a city obscured by a dense, black haze. "I should say that judging by the smoke we are now flying over Pittsburgh," one aviator declared. "No, Boy, That's Louisville," the other responded. "You know they DO see the sun once in a while in Pittsburgh."

Although observers have written about air pollution for decades and even centuries, not until recently did many people consider it a "problem" important enough to demand serious attention. In 1955, for example, *Louisville* magazine, a publication of the city's Chamber of Commerce, carried an article headlined "Air Pollution Standards, Opposed by Local Industry as 'Disastrous' to Some Firms, Postponed Indefinitely," in which the author smugly boasted that proposed pollution control regulations had been successfully "warded off." Three years later the *Courier-Journal* and the *Louisville Times*, both owned by the same publisher, ran an advertisement in the trade journal *Advertising Age* proudly proclaiming that the Ohio River Valley was "the Ruhr of America" and depicting a skyline of smokestacks belching soot into the atmosphere. For much of the nineteenth and twentieth centuries, such a view symbolized material growth and prosperity and the desired triumph of a progressive urban and industrial civilization over the savagery of untamed nature. Only after about 1960 had this image come to represent a deteriorating quality of life rather than a rising standard of living. As the newspapers' ed-

Metropolitan Louisville, looking toward the west across downtown and the West End

itors admitted in 1976, "those were the good old days, when Progress was partly defined by how sooty the air was, and we were euchered like nearly everyone else. A few people were trying to sound the alarm, but most Americans didn't start thinking seriously about the deterioration of our air and water until publication of Rachel Carson's *Silent Spring* in 1962."

Environmental problems associated with the automobile made some Americans of the late twentieth century nostalgic for the bygone days of the horse and buggy. They did not suspect, however, that their ancestors had blamed the horse for producing the same set of problems which they themselves attributed to the motor car: air contaminants harmful to the health, obnoxious odors, and disturbing noise. Historian Joel A. Tarr noted that "health officials in Rochester, New York, calculated in 1900 [that] the fifteen thousand horses in that city produced enough manure in a year to make a pile 175 feet high covering an acre of ground and breeding sixteen billion flies, each one a potential spreader of germs." Public health officials in cities across the country charged that wind-blown dust from pulverized manure damaged eyes and irritated respiratory organs, while the "noise and clatter" of city traffic aggravated nervous disorders.

By the turn of the century, writers in popular and scientific journals had begun to demand "the banishment" of the horse from American cities and to argue that the solution to the problem of urban transportation lay with the "horseless carriage." One authority predicted that the replacement of horses by motor vehicles would "benefit the public health to an almost incalculable degree," while another declared that "this crusade against the horse is a warfare of science against the visible unsanitation and the unseen pestilence of cities. The horse must make way for the motor." Some even promoted the automobile as a panacea for the physical and psychological problems which stemmed from the hectic pace of urban life. "It is the greatest health giving invention of a thousand years," publisher Frank A. Munsey exclaimed in 1903. "The cubic feet of fresh air that are literally forced into one while automobiling rehabilitate worn-out nerves and drive out worry, insomnia, and indigestion. It will renew the life and youth of the overworked man or woman, and will make the thin fat and the fat—but I forbear." Contemporaries did not consider mass transportation a particularly happy alternative to the horse. Nineteenth-century newspapers carried numerous complaints against the streetcars, railways, and trolleys, which pointed out that "people are packed into them like sardines in a box, with perspiration for oil," and that "ladies and gentlemen are compelled to sit down on seats sticky with nastiness, breathe loathsome air, and look out of cracked windows that are splashed with dirt from one end to the other." The generation of the turn of the century, then, hailed the automobile as a marvelous innovation which would at once solve the problems caused by the horse and by mass transit.

Late twentieth-century defenders of the city decried the exodus to the suburbs which the automobile had accelerated, little realizing that suburban growth had been an integral part of the process of urbanization for over 150 years. During the decades after 1830, mass transportation transformed compact "walking cities" into modern metropolises as the affluent moved to outlying "streetcar suburbs." Increasingly, rich and poor lived further apart, residential neighborhoods became remote from commercial and industrial districts, and the journey to work from house or apartment to office or factory became longer and more time consuming. Although post-World War II critics castigated the suburbs as sterile, child-centered enclaves of conformity, previous generations had celebrated suburban retreats as arcadian "middle landscapes" combining the best features of city and country life. In 1898 British planner Ebenezer Howard declared that "town and country *must be married,* and out of this joyous union will spring a new hope, a new life, a new civilization." Three years later Cornell University educator Liberty Hyde Bailey observed that "it is becoming more and more apparent that the ideal life is that which combines something of the social and intellectual advantages and physical comforts of the city with the inspiration and peaceful joys of the country." Most Americans applauded William Smythe in 1922 when he offered them "city homes on country lanes" combining "the cream of the country and the cream of the city, leaving the skim-milk for those who like that sort of thing."

Suburbanization appeared to many a new phenomenon after

1945 in part because, until fairly recently, suburbs simply did not *remain* suburbs for very long. Eager to enjoy urban services and to be incorporated into the larger community, most "streetcar suburbs" willingly gave up their separate identities and independent legal status and rapidly became urban neighborhoods. In consequence, city boundaries kept expanding and largely kept pace with population growth. The annexation of predominantly residential suburbs enabled Louisville, for example, to expand in area from five to sixty square miles during the hundred or so years after 1850. In the twentieth century, however, suburban resistance made annexation increasingly difficult, city boundaries stopped expanding, and urban populations began to level off and even decline. As historian Kenneth T. Jackson pointed out, "without exception, the adjustment of local boundaries has been the dominant method of population growth in every American city of consequence. . . . What was called the growth of Chicago or Philadelphia or Memphis was actually the building up of residential communities on their edges. . . . If annexation had not been successful in the nineteenth century, many large cities would have been surrounded by suburbs even before the Civil War." Viewed another way, had annexation continued to be successful in the twentieth century, the populations of cities like Louisville would have kept on growing. Indeed, during the 1970s, although the city of Louisville lost population, the Louisville metropolitan area continued to expand and suburban Oldham and Bullitt counties grew more rapidly than any other counties in the state.

After 1900, as suburbs increasingly elected to remain politically independent, metropolitan areas experienced governmental fragmentation. By 1979, there were within Jefferson County more than eighty incorporated municipalities and more than one hundred separate taxing authorities. A number of observers concluded that one or another form of metropolitan government offered the best alternative to annexation as a means of solving the problems of overlapping responsibilities and duplication of services. In 1972 the residents of Lexington and Fayette County voted to consolidate their city and county governments into a single, unified "urban county government." Political scientist W.E. Lyons concluded in 1977 that "after four years of operation, the

Lexington–Fayette Urban County Government is on the verge of fulfilling many of the promises made by the proponents of merger." Difficult problems remained to be solved, however, and the results of similar experiments in other cities were not overly encouraging. But by adding more than 65,000 residents to the Bluegrass city overnight, the consolidation of Lexington and Fayette County did help Lexington to become the fourth fastest-growing city in the United States during the 1970s.

The inability of cities to annex their suburbs in the twentieth century created severe financial strains on urban areas. As the affluent moved beyond municipal boundaries and as commercial and industrial activities relocated beyond corporate limits, cities had to contend with rising needs and shrinking tax bases. Commentators bemoaned the demise of the "self-sufficient city" capable of solving its own problems and the increasing need for municipalities to go hat-in-hand to the federal government for assistance. Yet, during the first decades of their history, the earliest cities in the Commonwealth had been anything but self-sufficient. Urban officials had to go "running down to Frankfort" to plead with state legislators for broadened powers, expanded city charters, and greater taxing authority in order to provide essential services and cope with mounting problems. Lexington's trustees complained in 1796 that they could not insure "the health, safety and convenience" of the town's inhabitants, while Louisville officials declared two decades later that their city's revenues were "entirely insufficient to answer the purposes of the town." A similar complaint was voiced early in the twentieth century. "The modern city has done its work and a change is coming," industrialist Henry Ford predicted in 1924. "The city has taught us much, but the overhead expense of living in such places is becoming unbearable. The cost of maintaining interest on debts, of keeping up water supply, sewerage and sanitary systems, the cost of traffic control and policing great masses of people are so great as to offset the benefits of the city. The cities are getting too heavy and are about doomed."

During the 1960s and 1970s urban planners and administrators struggled to revive older downtown areas and central business districts. In 1977 *Courier-Journal* reporter F.W. Woolsey suggested that Louisville's Main Street, after a prolonged slump, was "rebounding" as an entertainment and cultural center. "It was not until our era that Louisville turned toward the river instead of away" from it, Woolsey asserted. Yet fifty-six years earlier a writer for that same newspaper had proclaimed that "Main Street, like the old gray mare, ain't what she used to be. However, this fact will be related in paeans of joy tomorrow instead of in the plaintive tones appropriate to the case of the old gray mare." This 1921 account explained that Main Street, once Louisville's major wholesale district, had experienced a decline but was being rejuvenated. The writer observed that twenty-six firms had moved to Main Street during the previous two years, that a number of businesses which had been renting space had purchased property, and that there were only a few vacancies for sale or rent. Even though Main Street was thus revitalized in the 1920s and revitalized once again two generations later, at the end of the 1970s developers in Louisville as in other cities were still trying to pump new life into sluggish downtown areas with some combination of new performing arts centers, shopping complexes, sports arenas, convention centers, office and bank towers, and rehabilitated older structures. Officials could not agree, however, on what, if anything, could cure the problems of declining central business districts. A possible solution to these problems was unveiled one bright June day in 1978 when a former Miss Nudity International took a promotional stroll down Louisville's River City Mall to advertise her engagement at a local nightclub, "dressed in a scant green bikini, four-inch high heels and red hair." Proclaiming that "nudity is refreshing," she took the bikini off, prompting one excited onlooker to predict that "this will bring people back to the downtown area." Indeed, about one hundred spectators had gathered to observe the proceedings, but urban planners seemed uninterested in the possible implications for downtown revitalization.

Observers and preservationists complained during the 1970s that the historic fabric of cities was being demolished only to be replaced by monotonous, unimaginative, and unimpressive examples of contemporary architecture. They argued that the identities and personalities of cities suffered irreparable damage when distinctive older buildings designed by local architects and built by local craftsmen using locally available materials were replaced by modern office towers, apartment complexes, and shopping centers virtually indistinguishable from those put up elsewhere and everywhere. The editors of the *Courier-Journal* suggested in 1978 that Louisville had become the "Home of [the] Demolition Derby," and maintained that "for all the clamor . . . about preservationists' blocking progress, it's hard to recall a single case in Louisville in which a new building hasn't been built because history stood in the way. Bit by bit, our heritage is vanishing. The end of this will come when nothing worth preserving, or unique to Louisville, is left to fight for." Small numbers of urban residents had in fact been complaining for many decades about what Walt Whitman had termed the "pull-down-and-build-over spirit." In their 1967 study *A History of Urban America*, urban historians Charles N. Glaab and A. Theodore Brown dismissed the efforts of "traditionalists and others" who "sought to preserve structures which had been historically significant," and observed that "the thrust of American urbanization has always destroyed the old to make way for the new; urban development has always involved urban redevelopment."

During the 1970s, however, preservationists finally proved able to attract large audiences sympathetic to their point of view. Cities established landmark and historic preservation districts, residents formed neighborhood and city-wide preservation alliances, and Americans generally seemed to acquire a heightened appreciation of the value of significant architecture. In the second edition of *A History of Urban America*, published in 1976, Glaab and Brown revised their earlier view and admitted that "it had become increasingly clear that rebuilding in cities, judged by whatever set of values or standards one might choose, did not only represent change but also decline in the quality of craftsmanship and style in the urban building art." A report published in *Time* magazine in 1979 concluded that "if the past decade has produced a single cultural bench mark of note, it has been the remarkable turnabout in Americans' estimation of their bricks-and-mortar legacy."

By the 1970s, energy shortages, a faltering economy, and the environmentalist movement had all encouraged the "adaptive reuse" of highly prized and distinctive examples of local architecture. The emphasis in historic preservation had shifted away from "reverential restoration of old buildings" toward the modernization and reuse of these structures while maintaining their original character. "Several years ago, preservation meant restoration—making the old mansion into a museum, a monument to the past," Barbaralee Diamonstein of the New York City Landmarks Preservation Commission explained in 1978. "Today preservation does not, and emphatically should not, mean merely restoration. An important aspect of the preservation movement at present is the recycling of old buildings—adapting them to uses different from the ones for which they were originally intended." In Louisville, an old Greek Revival-style bank and the adjacent warehouse were adapted to house Actors Theatre, while a former dry goods store was redeveloped to serve as the home of a new Museum of History and Science.

During the 1960s it became fashionable to speak and to write about the "urban crisis," the "sick, sick cities," and the "death of the city." Author Norman Mailer pointed to a "middle-class lust for apocalypse," and Daniel P. Moynihan, formerly director of the Joint Center for Urban Studies of Harvard University and the Massachusetts Institute of Technology, argued in 1969 that the word "crisis" was "everywhere: on every tongue; in every pronouncement." Even an issue of *Glamour* magazine featured a beautiful black coed on the cover and posed the intriguing question: "The Urban Crisis: What Can One Girl Do?" Social critic Lewis Mumford wrote ominously of "necropolis," the city of the dead, and the "long, hot summers" of race riots during the mid-1960s inspired other cataclysmic visions. At the end of the 1970s, commentators continued to depict urban problems as intractable and overwhelming and to raise the specter of crisis and catastrophe. In 1978, for example, *Courier-Journal* columnist John Filiatreau pointed to the growing body of "doomsday" pronouncements regarding our polluted "urban wastelands" and declared that "in recent weeks I've seen four people wandering around downtown [Louisville] wearing surgical masks—an image that is fairly apocalyptic."

Yet even such cataclysmic visions, seemingly so appropriate to the late twentieth century, did not really represent a new development in the history of thought about urban life. During the late nineteenth century, the unexampled dislocations which accompanied urbanization, industrialization, and immigration generated analogous fears of impending catastrophe. In 1879 social critic Henry George, in his influential book *Progress and Poverty*, predicted that unless the harsher iniquities of urban and industrial life were soon remedied they would create "a despotism of the vilest and most degrading kind. . . . The sword will again be mightier than the pen, and . . . carnivals of destructive brute force and wild frenzy will alternate with the lethargy of a declining civilization." *Courier-Journal* editor Henry Watterson warned throughout these years that the conflict between Negro and white in the cities would eventually explode in a bloody "war of the races." In May 1886 a bomb was thrown into the midst of a group of policemen attempting to break up an anarchist rally in Chicago's Haymarket Square, and the incident sparked nightmares of revolutionary upheaval.

Only a month after the Haymarket affair an obscure writer named Caleb Ross published a lurid short story entitled "The Destruction of Louisville," which developed the idea that "the inevitable struggle between capital and labor" would end in carnage and devastation. "The handwriting had been written upon the wall of every city in the United States for years," Ross wrote somberly. "It needed but little prescience to see that we were standing upon the edge of a volcano." Peering into the abyss, Ross imagined that "the anarchists and communists who had been driven from New York and Chicago had fixed on Louisville as their point of rendezvous, and by careful management came into control of the labor organizations." In November 1887 the "bloodiest riots ever known in the history of the world" erupted. "Toward dusk we could see the flames shooting up in every direction from the beautiful residences that lined Third and Fourth streets south of Broadway." A little over a year later the city lay in ruins. "From a city of 180,000 inhabitants it has shrunk now to some 40,000 or 50,000. Away up Third and Fourth streets for miles there is a barren showing of blackened walls and eyeless windows. The grass is growing in the yards and on the sidewalks, and on Main Street only two or three feeble factories are endeavoring to sustain the ancient reputation of the city, but apparently in vain. The place seems to have a curse upon it. . . . The streets seem so desolate. . . . A death-like silence rests upon the place [which] was once the most flourishing city of the South. . . . The Louisville that is, how different from the Louisville that was!"

The cities "that are" do in fact differ greatly from the cities "that were," and in most respects they are better places in which to live. Urban residents in the late twentieth century lived longer and healthier lives than had previous generations, and enjoyed a quality of life and standard of living which their ancestors had only dreamed about. In terms of food, living space, creature comforts, and even personal security, the residents of contemporary cities could be considered far better off than their predecessors. "Considering the rapidity of urbanization in the United States since 1820, the failings of cities seem rather less significant than their accomplishments," urban historians Kenneth T. Jackson and Stanley K. Schultz concluded in 1972. "At no other time was so much—schools, houses, mass-transit facilities, sewers, factories, hospitals—built so rapidly for so many." Harvard University educator Edward C. Banfield, one of the more influential academic specialists in urban affairs and the former director of President Richard M. Nixon's Task Force on Model Cities, reached a similar conclusion in his controversial 1970 study *The Unheavenly City*. "The plain fact is that the overwhelming majority of city-dwellers live more comfortably and conveniently than ever before," he maintained. "By any conceivable measure of material welfare the present generation of urban Americans is, on the whole, better off than any other large group of people has ever been anywhere."

Banfield contended that the widespread alarm over a presumed urban crisis in the recent past stemmed neither from a failure to bring about reforms nor from a series of genuine emergencies. He argued rather that Americans believed in the existence of an urban crisis because "the improvements in performance, great as they have been, have not kept pace with rising expectations. In other words, although things have been getting better absolutely, they have been getting worse *relative to what we think they should be*. . . . To a large extent, then, our urban problems are like the mechanical rabbit at the racetrack, which is set to keep just ahead of the dogs no matter how fast they may run. Our performance is better and better, but because we set our standards and expectations to keep ahead of performance, the problems are never any nearer to solution. Indeed, if standards and expectations rise *faster* than performance, the problems may get (relatively) worse as they get (absolutely) better."

Banfield's conclusions have been widely challenged and debated, and at the end of the 1970s there was little agreement about the state of the cities or about their future prospects. What did seem clear was that American and Kentucky cities had weathered many "crises." They had served as dynamic agents of modernization, spearheading advances in economic, social, and cultural life. They had provided a vital "safety valve" for economically distressed agricultural areas and small towns. They had made a "good life" with a high standard of living possible for an increasingly large proportion of the population. And they had continued to represent, in the words of the municipal reformer Frederic C. Howe, "the hope of democracy." In 1906 Howe had written that "the city has become the central feature in modern civilization and to an ever increasing extent the dominant one." In 1980 the city remained the central and dominant feature of our civilization and continued to perform its classical civilizing functions in the Commonwealth as throughout America. The attractions of urban life remained as powerful as they had been at the turn of the century, when journalist Finley Peter Dunne's fictional bartender-philosopher Martin J. Dooley had spoken in his thick Irish brogue of the compelling lure of the city. "Ye might say as Hogan does, that we're ladin' an artyficyal life," Mr. Dooley declared, "but, be Hivins, ye might as well tell me I ought to be paradin' up and down a hillside in a suit iv skins, shootin' the antylope an' the moose, be gory, an' livin' in a cave as to make me believe I ought to get along without sthreet cars an' ilictric lights an' illyvators an' sody wather an' ice. 'We ought to live where all the good things iv life comes from,' says Hogan. 'No,' says I. 'Th' place to live is where all the good things iv life goes to.'"

Bibliographical Note

The following selection of books, articles, and theses is primarily intended to provide a guide to the works I found particularly valuable and upon which I relied most heavily. It is secondarily intended to serve as a guide to further reading.

The great majority of the works cited contain detailed references to other published studies and to the wide range of primary sources which pertain to the urban history of Kentucky.

In the interest of brevity, items are referred to only once, even though a particular source may have proven useful in the writing of two or more chapters. The *Filson Club History Quarterly* and the *Register of the Kentucky Historical Society* are abbreviated *FCHQ* and *RKHS*, respectively.

Chapter 1

Richard C. Wade, *The Urban Frontier: The Rise of Western Cities, 1790-1830* (Cambridge, 1959), is a landmark history of urbanization in the Ohio Valley and is indispensable for the study of all aspects of society and life in early Louisville and Lexington.

The best modern overview of the history of Louisville is George H. Yater, *Two Hundred Years at the Falls of the Ohio: A History of Louisville and Jefferson County* (Louisville, 1979). A good account of the city's early history is Elizabeth Walker Chenault, "The Development of Louisville, Town and City, from the Earliest Beginnings to 1830" (M.A. thesis, University of Louisville, 1962). The following older histories are still useful: Henry McMurtrie, *Sketches of Louisville and Its Environs* (Louisville, 1819); Ben Casseday, *The History of Louisville, from Its Earliest Settlement till the Year 1852* (Louisville, 1852); [Henry A. Ford and Kate B. Ford], *History of the Ohio Falls Cities and Their Counties*, 2 vols. (Cleveland, 1882); and J. Stoddard Johnston, ed., *Memorial History of Louisville from Its First Settlement to the Year 1896*, 2 vols. (Chicago, [1896]).

The early history of Lexington is described in George W. Ranck, *History of Lexington, Kentucky: Its Early Annals and Recent Progress* (Cincinnati, 1872); Charles R. Staples, *The History of Pioneer Lexington, Kentucky, 1779-1806* (Lexington, Ky., 1939); Lee Shai Weissbach, "The Peopling of Lexington, Kentucky" (manuscript); and Harriet Belt Glascock, "Lexington: A Cultural Center in the Eighteenth Century West" (M.A. thesis, University of Kentucky, 1928). An especially enlightening essay is Bernard Mayo, "Lexington: Frontier Metropolis," in Eric F. Goldman, ed., *Historiography and Urbanization: Essays in American History in Honor of W. Stull Holt* (Baltimore, 1941), 21-42.

Amusing and informative accounts of early promotional activities include Mariam S. Houchens, "Three Kentucky Towns that Never Were," *FCHQ* 40 (January 1966): 17-21; Robert D. Arbuckle, "Ohiopiomingo: The 'Mythical' Kentucky Settlement that Was Not a Myth," *RKHS* 70 (October 1972): 318-24; Walter Havighurst, *Wilderness for Sale: The Story of the First Western Land Rush* (New York, 1956); John W. Reps, *The Making of Urban America: A History of City Planning in the United States* (Princeton, 1965), especially 352-58; and Charles N. Glaab, "Historical Perspective on Urban Development Schemes," in Leo F. Schnore and Henry Fagin, eds., *Urban Research and Policy Planning* (Beverly Hills, 1967), 197-219.

An excellent introduction to American urban history which has strongly influenced my thinking is Charles N. Glaab and A. Theodore Brown, *A History of Urban America*, 2nd ed. (New York, 1976; 1st ed., 1967). See also Howard P. Chudacoff, *The Evolution of American Urban Society*, 2nd ed. (Englewood Cliffs, N.J., 1981; 1st ed., 1975).

Chapter 2

Urban promotion in early Kentucky is described in Stuart Seely Sprague, "Town Making in the Era of Good Feelings: Kentucky, 1814-1820," *RKHS* 72 (October 1974): 337-41, an article which captures the exuberance of town booming written by a careful student of Kentucky history. The significance of urban boosterism is provocatively examined in Daniel J. Boorstin, *The Americans: The National Experience* (New York, 1965), part 3, "The Upstarts: Boosters," 113-68.

Information relating to Lexington's economic and cultural development during the period is contained in T.D. Clark, "The Lexington and Ohio Railroad—A Pioneer Venture," *RKHS* 31 (January 1933): 9-28; James F. Hopkins, *A History of the Hemp Industry in Kentucky* (Lexington, Ky., 1951); Niels Henry Sonne, *Liberal Kentucky, 1780-1828* (New York, 1939), a particularly important work; and the early chapters of John D. Wright, Jr., *Transylvania: Tutor to the West* (Lexington, Ky., 1975).

Louisville's maturation and economic growth are examined in James Parker Oliver, "A History of the Canal Projects at the Falls of the Ohio River" (M.A. thesis, University of Kentucky, 1937); Paul Fatout, "Canal Agitation at Ohio Falls," *Indiana Magazine of History* 57 (December 1961): 279-309; Stuart Seely Sprague, "The Canal at the Falls of the Ohio and the Three Cornered Rivalry," *RKHS* 72 (January 1974): 38-54; Carl E. Kramer, "Images of a Developing City: Louisville, 1800-1830," *FCHQ* 52 (April 1978): 166-90; Ann Brown Matheny, "Some Aspects of Life in Louisville during the 1840's" (M.A. thesis, University of Kentucky, 1958); James Sullivan, "Louisville's Civic and Business Advancements in the Rioting Decade, 1850-1860" (M.A. thesis, University of Louisville, 1958); Maury Klein, *History of the Louisville & Nashville Railroad* (New York, 1972); and Charles Messmer, "Louisville on the Eve of the Civil War," *FCHQ* 50 (July 1976): 249-89. A good study of the impact of Louisville's expansion on a neighboring city is Victor M. Bogle, "New Albany within the Shadow of Louisville," *Indiana Magazine of History* 51 (December 1955): 303-16.

Railroad developments are treated in William B. Graham, "Railroads in Kentucky before 1860" (M.A. thesis, University of Kentucky, 1931); Carl B. Boyd, Jr., "Local Aid to Railroads in Central Kentucky, 1850-1891," *RKHS* 62 (January and April 1964): 4-23, 112-33; and Stuart Seely Sprague, "Kentucky and the Cincinnati-Charleston Railroad, 1835-1839," *RKHS* 73 (April 1975): 122-35.

Chapter 3

Several studies describe the rise of urban problems and the development of urban services in early nineteenth-century Kentucky. On fire protection see John B. Clark, Jr., "From Bucket Brigade to Steam Fire Engine: Fire Fighting in Old Louisville through 1865," *FCHQ* 27 (April 1953): 103-18; and Clark, "The Fire Problem in Kentucky, 1778-1865: A Case History of the Ante-Bellum South," *RKHS* 51 (April 1953): 97-122. Studies of disease and public health include Nancy D. Baird, "Asiatic Cholera's First Visit to Kentucky: A Study in Panic and Fear," *FCHQ* 48 (July 1974): 228-40; Baird, "Asiatic Cholera: Kentucky's First Public Health Instructor," *FCHQ* 48 (October 1974): 327-41; and Katherine H. Bottigheimer, "Origin and Early Functioning of the Health Department of Louisville in Kentucky, 1792-1850" (seminar paper, University of Louisville, 1968). There is also useful information in F. Garvin Davenport, *Ante-Bellum Kentucky: A Social History, 1800-1860* (Oxford, Ohio, 1943), chapter 2, "Life in Town," 21-36; and Clement Eaton, *The*

Growth of Southern Civilization, 1790-1860 (New York, 1961), chapter 11, "Town Life," 247-70.

Broader studies include James F. Richardson, *Urban Police in the United States* (Port Washington, N.Y., 1974); Nelson Manfred Blake, *Water for the Cities: A History of the Urban Water Supply Problem in the United States* (Syracuse, 1956); Lawrence H. Larsen, "Nineteenth-Century Street Sanitation: A Study of Filth and Frustration," *Wisconsin Magazine of History* 52 (Spring 1969): 239-47; and Charles E. Rosenberg, *The Cholera Years: The United States in 1832, 1849, and 1866* (Chicago, 1962).

Chapter 4

An excellent case study of the Louisville-Cincinnati trade rivalry is Leonard P. Curry, *Rail Routes South: Louisville's Fight for the Southern Market, 1865-1872* (Lexington, Ky., 1969). Curry places this controversy within a provocative theoretical framework in his article "Urban Mercantilism in Mid-Nineteenth Century America" (manuscript). Louisville's economic development is also dealt with in James P. Sullivan, "Louisville and Her Southern Alliance, 1865-1890" (Ph.D. dissertation, University of Kentucky, 1965); Jesse C. Burt, Jr., "Edmund W. Cole and the Struggle between Nashville and Louisville and Their Railroads, 1879-1880," *FCHQ* 26 (April 1952): 112-32; and Ernest J. Hopkins, *The Louisville Industrial Foundation: A Study in Community Capitalization of Local Industries* (Atlanta, 1945). Jean Howerton Coady tells the story of the Louisville Booster Car in "Nostalgic Odyssey," *Courier-Journal & Times Magazine* (May 22, 1977), 21-24. Keith L. Bryant, Jr., provides a context for appreciating the historical significance of Louisville's Union Station in "Cathedrals, Castles, and Roman Baths: Railway Station Architecture in the Urban South," *Journal of Urban History* 2 (February 1976): 195-230.

A good account of Owensboro's promotional efforts is Lee A. Dew, "Owensboro's Dream of Glory: A Railroad to Russellville," *FCHQ* 52 (January 1978): 26-45. Urban growth in the mountains of Kentucky is treated in D.H. Davis, "Urban Development in the Kentucky Mountains," *Annals of the Association of American Geographers* 15 (June 1925): 92-99; Stuart Seely Sprague, "The Great Appalachian Iron and Coal Town Boom of 1889-1893," *Appalachian Journal* 4 (Spring-Summer 1977): 216-23; Charles Blanton Roberts, "The Building of Middlesborough—A Notable Epoch in Eastern Kentucky History," *FCHQ* 7 (January 1933): 18-33; John Gaventa, *Power and Powerlessness: Qui-*

escence and Rebellion in an Appalachian Valley (Urbana, Ill., 1980), chapter 3, "The Impact of Industrial Power: The Shaping of a Company Valley," 47-83, an interpretive account of Middlesboro's "boom" and "bust"; and Thomas A. Kelemen, "A History of Lynch, Kentucky, 1917-1930," *FCHQ* 48 (April 1974): 156-76.

A comprehensive overview of this period of American urban history is Blake McKelvey, *The Urbanization of America, 1860-1915* (New Brunswick, N.J., 1963).

Chapter 5

Richard C. Wade, *Slavery in the Cities: The South, 1820-1860* (New York, 1964), is an original and provocative treatment of a neglected subject. An interesting statistical analysis which takes issue with some of Wade's conclusions is Claudia Dale Goldin, *Urban Slavery in the American South, 1820-1860: A Quantitative History* (Chicago, 1976).

The relationship between race relations and American minstrelsy is examined in James H. Dormon, "The Strange Career of Jim Crow Rice (with apologies to Professor Woodward)," *Journal of Social History* 3 (Winter 1969-1970): 109-22. Two studies with information on Lexington's black community are Herbert A. Thomas, Jr., "Victims of Circumstance: Negroes in a Southern Town, 1865-1880," *RKHS* 71 (July 1973): 253-71; and John Kellogg, "Negro Urban Clusters in the Postbellum South," *Geographical Review* 67 (July 1977): 310-21.

The history of race relations in Louisville after 1865 is covered in Zane L. Miller, "Urban Blacks in the South, 1865-1920: The Richmond, Savannah, New Orleans, Louisville and Birmingham Experience," in Leo F. Schnore, ed., *The New Urban History: Quantitative Explorations by American Historians* (Princeton, 1975), 184-204; Judith Walzer [Leavitt], "Segregation in Louisville, 1867-1890" (seminar paper, University of Chicago, 1966); Marjorie M. Norris, "An Early Instance of Nonviolence: The Louisville Demonstrations of 1870-1871," *Journal of Southern History* 32 (November 1966): 487-504; George Carlton Wright, "Blacks in Louisville, Kentucky, 1890-1930" (Ph.D. dissertation, Duke University, 1977); Darlene Walker Eakin, "Preparation for the Desegregation of the Louisville School System" (M.A. thesis, University of Louisville, 1974); John Marshall Thompson, "School Desegregation in Jefferson County, Kentucky, 1954-1975" (Ed.D. dissertation, University of Kentucky, 1976); "Is 'Voluntary' Integration the Answer?" *U.S. News & World Report* 41 (October 5, 1956): 46-56, 142-49; Omer Carmichael and Weldon James, *The Louisville Story* (New York, 1957); George C. Wright, "Desegregation of Public Accommodations in Louisville, Kentucky: A Long and Difficult Struggle in a 'Liberal' Border City" (manuscript); Hunter S. Thompson, "A Southern City with Northern Problems," in *The Great Shark Hunt: Strange Tales from a Strange Time* (New York, 1979), 38-46, originally published in 1963; Roger M. Williams, "What Louisville Has Taught Us about Busing," *Saturday Review* 4 (April 30, 1977): 6-10, 51; and Regina M. Monsour, "The Political Efficacy of Lyman Tefft Johnson" (M.A. thesis, University of Louisville, 1978).

Three valuable interpretive essays are Zane L. Miller, "The Black Experience in the Modern American City," in Raymond A. Mohl and James F. Richardson, eds., *The Urban Experience: Themes in American History* (Belmont, Cal., 1973), 44-60; Richard C. Wade, "Historical Analogies and Public Policy: The Black and Immigrant Experience in Urban America," in Robert F. Oaks et al., *Essays on Urban America* (Austin, 1975), 127-47; and Harvard Sitkoff, "Race Relations: Progress and Prospects," in James T. Patterson, ed., *Paths to the Present: Interpretive Essays on American History since 1930* (Minneapolis, 1975), 183-227.

Chapter 6

The cultural life of modern Louisville and the history of the Louisville Orchestra are examined in George R. Leighton, "Louisville, Kentucky: An American Museum Piece," *Harper's Magazine* 175 (September 1937): 400-421; William Manchester, "Louisville Cashes In on Culture," *Harper's Magazine* 211 (August 1955): 77-83; "Culture's New Kentucky Home," *Life* 42 (April 8, 1957): 125-30; Fred Powledge, "City in Transition," *New Yorker* 50 (September 9, 1974): 42-83; Carole C. Birkhead, "The History of the Orchestra in Louisville" (M.A. thesis, University of Louisville, 1977); Robert S. Whitney, "In Retrospect: The First Thirty Years of the Louisville Orchestra, 1937-1967" (manuscript); and Philip Hart, *Orpheus in the New World: The Symphony Orchestra as an American Cultural Institution* (New York, 1973), chapter 9, "Louisville Orchestra," 192-211. The value of the performing arts to the economic vitality of modern cities is the theme of *The Taxpayers' Revolt and the Arts: A U.S. Conference of Mayors' Position Paper* (Washington, D.C., [1978]).

Chapter 7

The history of change and continuity in urban life is reflected in Sam Bass Warner, Jr., *The Private City: Philadelphia in Three Periods of Its Growth* (Philadelphia, 1968); Blake McKelvey, *The Emergence of Metro-*

politan America, 1915-1966 (New Brunswick, N.J., 1968); H.J. Dyos, "Some Historical Reflections on the Quality of Urban Life," in Henry J. Schmandt and Warner Bloomberg, Jr., eds., *The Quality of Urban Life* (Beverly Hills, 1969), 31-60; Otto L. Bettmann, *The Good Old Days— They Were Terrible!* (New York, 1974); Martin V. Melosi, ed., *Pollution and Reform in American Cities, 1870-1930* (Austin, 1980); Joel A. Tarr, "Urban Pollution—Many Long Years Ago," *American Heritage* 22 (October 1971): 65-69, 106; Glen E. Holt, "The Changing Perception of Urban Pathology: An Essay on the Development of Mass Transit in the United States," in Kenneth T. Jackson and Stanley K. Schultz, eds., *Cities in American History* (New York, 1972), 324-43; Peter J. Schmitt, *Back to Nature: The Arcadian Myth in Urban America* (New York, 1969); Kenneth T. Jackson, "Metropolitan Government Versus Suburban Autonomy: Politics on the Crabgrass Frontier," in Jackson and Schultz, *Cities in American History*, 442-62; W.E. Lyons, *The Politics of City-County Merger: The Lexington-Fayette County Experience* (Lexington, Ky., 1977); Richard C. Wade, "The End of the Self-Sufficient City: New York's Fiscal Crisis in History," *Urbanism Past & Present* 3 (Winter 1976-1977): 1-4; F.W. Woolsey, "Louisville's Rebounding Main [Street]," *Courier-Journal & Times Magazine* (September 11, 1977), 14-21; Barbaralee Diamonstein, *Buildings Reborn: New Uses, Old Places* (New York, 1978); Caleb Ross, "The Destruction of Louisville," *Southern Bivouac* n.s. 2 (June 1886): 49-58; Edward C. Banfield, *The Unheavenly City: The Nature and Future of Our Urban Crisis* (Boston, 1968, 1970); Daniel P. Moynihan, "The Soulless City," *American Heritage* 20 (February 1969): 5-8, 78-85; James C. Starbuck, "The Use and Abuse of the American City" (St. Louis, 1973); James F. Richardson, "Perspectives on the Contemporary City," in Mohl and Richardson, *The Urban Experience*, 222-38; and Richard C. Wade, "America's Cities Are (Mostly) Better Than Ever," *American Heritage* 30 (February/March 1979): 4-13.

Index

Actors Theatre of Louisville, 119-21, 137
Air pollution, 128-32
Annexation, 45, 133-34
Appalachia, town boom in, 80-83
Architecture, 77-78, 135-37
Ashland, 44, 83, 125-26
Automobiles, 125-26, 128-32

Barbourville, 79
Bardstown, 16, 43, 123
Benham, 80
Berea, 123
Boosterism. *See* Urban promotion
Bowling Green, 37, 43-44

Calais, 23
Carrollton, 44
Catlettsburg, 44, 83
Cholera, 61-65
Cincinnati: rivalry with Lexington, 28-30; rivalry with Louisville, 30, 33-35, 38-39, 66-73; rivalry with other Kentucky cities, 39-40
Cincinnati Southern Railroad, 37, 72, 76
City: concepts of and attitudes toward, 7-8, 20, 123; lure of the, 79, 140
Clarksville, Ind., 17
Columbia, 64-65
Columbus, 44
Commerce, 3-6, 9-10, 17, 31-33, 36, 66-73
Corbin, 79, 82
Covington, 16, 39-41, 44, 47, 63, 79, 125-26
Crime, 12, 55-56
Culture, 7-8, 12, 15, 27-31, 109-22

Danville, 16, 62, 73
Dawson Springs, 79
Dover, 23

Elba, 23
Elizabethtown, 43, 71, 73, 125
Elkhorn City, 79
Epidemics and disease, 4, 60-65; stagnant pools of water related to, 4, 60
Evansville, Ind., 71, 73, 75, 126

Falls of the Ohio, 1-3, 6, 17, 33-36, 47
Farnsley, Charles P., 110-12, 115-18, 121
Fire protection, 58-59
Francesburg, 23
Frankfort, 16, 39, 44
Franklin, 43-44
Franklinville, 18-19, 25
Fulton, 79

Georgetown, 16
Ghent, 22
Glasgow, 37, 43
Greensburg, 73
Greenville, 79

Harlan, 79
Hazard, 79
Health protection, 61-65
Henderson, 44, 60, 71, 73, 126
Hickman, 44
Historic preservation, 135-37
Hopkinsville, 44, 126
Housing, 5, 7, 11-12, 96-98
Hygeia, 25

Indians, 2, 4, 9, 17
Industry, 6, 10-11, 33, 76-77, 80, 86-87

Jeffersonville, Ind., 17, 34-36, 41
Jenkins, 79-80
Johnson, Lyman T., 99, 103, 106, 108
Jory, Jon, 120

Lancaster, 123
Lawrenceburg, 123
Lexington: commerce, 9-10; culture, 12, 15, 27-31; epidemics and disease, 62-65; fire protection, 58-59; founding, 9; growth, 9-12, 15, 26-27, 123-24, 126, 134; health protection, 61-65; housing, 11-12; images of, 26-29; industry, 10-11; mobility, 13-14; Negroes, 56, 58, 89, 91; planning, 18; police protection, 56-57; politics and government, 133-34; population, 9, 11, 15, 26-27, 125, 134; real estate values, 12, 26; rivalry with Cincinnati, 28-30; rivalry with Louisville, 26, 28-31, 72; sanitation, 52-54; schools, 12, 27, 31; slavery, 89, 91; social life, 12-14, 26-29; street cleaning, paving, and repair, 12, 50-54; street lighting, 54-55; suburbs, 123; transportation, 51-52
Living standards: elite, 14-15, wage earners, 13-14
Louisville: air pollution, 128-32; architecture, 77-78, 136-37; commerce, 4-6, 31-33, 36, 66-73; culture, 7, 109-22; descriptions and images, 4-5, 38, 60, 68-70, 138-39; desegregation, 99-108; epidemics and disease, 4, 60-65; fire protection, 58-59; founding, 3; growth, 4-7, 31-33, 76-77, 133; health protection, 61-65; housing, 5, 7, 96-98; industry, 6, 33, 76-77, 86-87; Negroes, 56, 58, 88-108; noise pollution, 127-28; planning, 18, 47; police protection, 50, 56-57; politics and government, 48-50, 134; population, 5-6, 31, 38-39, 46-47; promotion, 1-2, 38, 66-67, 77, 86-87; real estate values, 7; rivalry with Cincinnati, 30, 33-35, 38-39, 66-73; rivalry with Covington, 40-41; rivalry with Jeffersonville, Ind., 35-36; rivalry with Lexington, 26, 28-31, 72; rivalry with Nashville, 36-37, 74-75; rivalry with New Albany, Ind., 17, 41-43; sanitation, 52-54, 131; schools, 8, 95, 99, 101-03, 106-07; segregation, 92-108; slavery, 88-92; social life, 7; street cleaning, paving, and repair, 50-54; street lighting, 54-55; suburbs, 47-48, 96, 133; transportation, 51-52, 95-97; water supply, 59-60
Louisville and Nashville Railroad, 36-37, 43-44, 70-73, 75-76, 82; Union Station, 77, 93
Louisville and Portland Canal, 36
Louisville Booster Car, 87
Louisville, Cincinnati & Charleston Railroad, 39-40
Louisville Industrial Foundation, 86-87
Louisville Orchestra, 110-19
Lynch, 79-80
Lystra, 18-19, 25

Madisonville, 44
Manchester, 22
Marion, 22
Mayfield, 79
Maysville, 16, 39-40, 44
Middlesboro, 79, 81-83
Midway, 23
Minerva, 23
Mobility, 13-14
Morehead, 123
Morganfield, 79
Morganza, 23
Mount Vernon, 71
Municipal government, 3, 14, 48-50, 76, 133-34
Murray, 79

Nashville, Tenn., 36-37, 43-44, 74-75
Nashville, Chattanooga and St. Louis Railroad, 74-75
National Advisory Commission on Civil Disorders, 106-07
Negroes, 56, 58, 88-108

149

New Albany, Ind., 17, 41-43
New Haven, 43
Newport, 16, 40-41, 44, 47, 79, 125-26

Ohiopiomingo, 19, 25
Owensboro, 44, 47, 73-74, 126
Owensboro and Russellville Railroad, 73-74

Paducah, 44, 47, 71, 125
Paintsville, 79
Palermo, 23
Paris, 16, 22
Pikeville, 79
Pineville, 79
Planning, 18-19, 47
Police protection, 50, 56-57
Politics: urban-rural antagonism, 48-50. *See also* Municipal government
Pollution: air, 128-32; noise, 127-28
Portland, 16-17, 23, 42, 45, 47, 51
Poverty, 94
Prestonsburg, 79
Princeton, 79
Providence, 79

Radcliff, 125
Ragarsville, 23
Railroads, 36-40, 43-44, 70-76
Real estate: speculation, 14, 17-19, 22-25, 80-85; values, 7, 11, 26
Richmond, 71
Ripley, 23
Russellville, 23, 44, 62, 73

Sanitation, 52-54, 131
Savannah, 23
Schools, 8, 12, 27-31, 95, 99, 101-03, 106-07
Scottsville, 43
Segregation, 92-108
Shelbyville, 16
Shippingport, 16-17, 23, 45, 47
Slavery, 56, 58, 89-92
Social life, 7, 12-13, 26-29
Somerset, 72, 79
Standard Metropolitan Statistical Areas, 126
Stanford, 71-72

Steamboats, 21; damage economy of Lexington, 15-16, 26-27; stimulate economy of Louisville, 31, 36
Stearns, 80
Street maintenance: cleaning, paving, and repair, 12, 50-54; lighting, 54-55
Sturgis, 79
Suburbanization, 47-48, 125-26, 132-33

Transportation: horses v. automobiles, 131-32; intra-urban, 51-52, 95-96; railroads, 36-40, 43-44, 70-76
Transylvania, 23
Transylvania University, 12, 27-31

Urban crisis, 46, 126-27, 137-40
Urban promotion (boosterism), 1-2, 17-19, 22-25, 31, 66-67, 72-73, 77, 80-87
Urban revitalization, 134-35
Urban rivalry, 25-26, 39-40, 43-45, 125; Lexington v. Cincinnati, 28-30; Louisville v. Cincinnati, 30, 33-35, 38-39, 66-73; Louisville v. Covington, 40-41; Louisville v. Jeffersonville, Ind., 35-36; Louisville v. Lexington, 26, 28-31, 72; Louisville v. Nashville, 36-37, 74-75; Louisville v. New Albany, Ind., 17, 41-43
Urban-rural antagonism, 20-21
Urbanization: attitudes toward, 79, 123; in Kentucky, 2, 16, 43-44, 79-80, 123-25
Utica, 22

Van Lear, 79
Versailles, 16, 22

Water supply, 59-60
Watterson, Henry, 69, 74, 76-77, 85, 93, 95-96, 138
Wayland, 79
Whitney, Robert S., 110-19
Williamsburg, 79
Wilmore, 123
Winchester, 81

www.ingramcontent.com/pod-product-compliance
Lightning Source LLC
Chambersburg PA
CBHW032049150426
43194CB00006B/471